Intrepid Journeys

Juliet Coombe
Elliot Daniel
Steve Davey
Josie Dew
Craig Dixon
Mike Gerrard
Mark Hodson
Lyn Hughes
Ian Jackson
Peter Robinson
Anna Rockall

Edited by: Ramona Khambatta

La Belle Aurore

First published in Great Britain in 1998 by
La Belle Aurore
15 Ballater Road
London SW2 5QS
Tel: 0171-924 0856

Intrepid Journeys © La Belle Aurore 1998

The right of La Belle Aurore to be associated as the authors of this work has been asserted by them in accordance with the Copyright Designs and Patents Act 1988.

Stories © the individual writers.

The right of the individual writers to be associated as the authors of their stories has been asserted by them in accordance with the Copyright Designs and Patents Act 1988.

ISBN 0 9534423 0 6

Editor: Ramona Khambatta

Concept and Finance: Juliet Coombe

Design and Production: Steve Davey

Cover montage: Steve Davey

With photographs by: Steve Davey and Juliet Coombe

Printed by: Chromo Litho (01244-347544)

This book is sold subject to the condition that it shall not, by way of trade or otherwise, be lent, resold, hired out or otherwise circulated without the publisher's prior written consent in any form of binding other than that in which it is published and without a similar condition including this condition being imposed upon the subsequent publisher.

Contents

The Writers 4
Introduction *Darrell Wade* 7
Vietnam: Russia's Greatest Love Machine *Ian Jackson* 9
Laos: From Arms To Alms *Juliet Coombe* 23
Thailand: The Spirit Of The Naga *Elliot Daniel* 33
Sumatra: Going Ape In Sumatra *Mike Gerrard* 43
China: On The Road To Lhasa *Steve Davey* 55
Burma: Sucking Eggs In Burma *Peter Robinson* 67
Cambodia: Temples In the Jungle *Juliet Coombe* 77
Philippines: A Bus To Batad *Mark Hodson* 87
Indonesia: Trouble On Paradise Island *Anna Rockall* 97
India: Going Naked At The Mela *Steve Davey* 107
Thailand: Taking The Trunk Road *Lyn Hughes* 117
Burma: Waking To Dreams Of Monglar *Juliet Coombe* 127
Vietnam: Where The Dragon Descends To The Sea *Craig Dixon* .. 139
China: A Romantic Landslide In China: *Ian Jackson* 149
Borneo: Climbing Out Of The Jungle *Steve Davey* 157
Japan: Riding A Typhoon On Ishigaki *Josie Dew* 165

The Writers

Juliet Coombe
Juliet Coombe, co-founder of La Belle Aurore, began her career at the age of 17 as a photojournalist. She was deported from Malawi for wearing trousers; put in prison in Zambia because the police thought she was a South African spy; and ate dog in Vietnam by accident. Her mishaps have provided endless entertainment for readers of Wanderlust, TNT Magazine, and Time Out, some of the publications that she freelances for. Unsurprisingly, her latest project is a TV series called 'Hot Spots'.

Elliot Daniel
Elliot Daniel is a tour guide for Intrepid Travel and has worked and explored extensively throughout Southeast Asia for the past three years. He is a freelance photojournalist and presenter of travel documentaries. He has an honours degree in tourism and is currently researching the effects of 'hilltribe tourism' across Southeast Asia in an attempt to answer the question, 'Can tourism be a form of sustainable development?', for his PhD.

Steve Davey
Steve Davey is a founding partner of La Belle Aurore. He has spent many years travelling, writing and 'looking for excitement'. As well as being a photographer and a writer he has been the editor of two magazines and has contributed to the Digital Photographer's Handbook. He has driven across deserts, hiked up mountains to film gorillas, been bitten by a lion, visited festivals all over the world, run with bulls, bungy-jumped and brought his unique view of the world to many features.

The Writers

Jose Dew
Josie Dew has spent 15 years cycling in fits and starts around the world. 200,000 miles, 41 countries, five continents, a lot of wobbly legs and a handful of punctures later she is still to be found firmly fixed to the saddle. To finance her trips, Josie has published two books 'The Winds In My Wheels' and 'Travels In A Strange State'. The story published in this book is an extract from 'A Ride In The Neon Sun', published on 1 April 1999 by Little Brown.

Craig Dixon
Born in Victoria and raised in Queensland, Craig left high school at 16 to work as a copyboy on the local newspaper. After becoming a graded journalist, he resigned to go 'on the wallaby' around Australia. That was the beginning of a chronic wanderlust. A three-month trip to Thailand and Vietnam convinced Craig and his fiancee to throw in bright careers at Australia's biggest-selling daily newspaper to travel the world. That was three years ago and he's no closer to returning home.

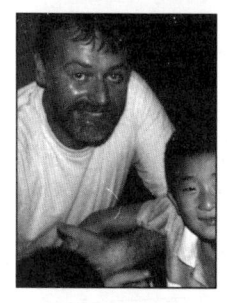

Mike Gerrard
Mike Gerrard is a British travel writer whose work has appeared in newspapers and magazines around the world. He has won an Award for Excellence for Photojournalism from the Outdoor Writers' Guild of Great Britain, and a Travelex Travel Writer's Award for a piece he wrote about Yangshuo in China.

Mark Hodson
Mark Hodson quit his job as a newspaper sub-editor to spend 18 months travelling around Asia and Latin America. He has worked in New York, Hong Kong and the Bahamas and now lives in London where he writes on travel for The Sunday Times. Mark is the author of World Wise: Your Passport to Safer Travel (Thomas Cook, £6.99).

Lyn Hughes
Lyn Hughes once had a well-paid and demanding career with a multi-national company. Plagued by the 'wanderlust', she gave it all up to travel the world. In 1993 she co-founded and became Editor of Wanderlust magazine aimed at people with an insatiable passion for travel. The magazine has gone from strength to strength. Lyn is a member of the British Guild of Travel Writers, and contributes to other publications, to radio and TV.

Ian Jackson
En route to London, Ian Jackson spent 18 months in South East Asia. He got intimately acquainted with squat bogs in China, Vietnam, Thailand, Laos, Malaysia and Indonesia and travelled by boat, bus, train, horse, motorbike, truck, foot and countless other bizzare forms of transport. On his arrival in London he became travel editor and later editor of TNT Magazine, a leading publication for travellers and Australasians in the UK.

Peter Robinson
Born in Melbourne, Australia, Peter still lives in its seaside suburb of Brighton. He has travelled through outback Australia, Europe, north Africa and the South Pacific, but in recent years has focussed his lenses on Asia. His work is seen regularly in the Melbourne Herald Sun, Expanse travel magazine, Weekends for Two, Overlander 4WD magazine, and his work has appeared in scores of Australian publications in the last decade.

Anna Rockall
Anna is a freelance journalist based in London. She has published travel pieces in the Independent, FHM and Time Out amongst others. Anna's main love is for the wilderness and the remoter corners of the globe; her favourite part of travelling is when you look around and realise that you are in the middle of nowhere. She dislikes having to be wary of strange men and finding scary spiders in her belongings. She would like to be a proper explorer, but fears she isn't quite hard enough.

Introduction

An Intrepid Journey can mean many different things to different people. To me it means just one thing – to travel outside your comfort zone. An Intrepid Journey does not have to be physically challenging or emotionally draining, but it does have to open your eyes to a new world and a different way of doing things. It has to challenge your preconceptions and in some way, change the way you think. It is a journey that leaves something of itself in your mind forever, though you may never be quite sure what it is. You are holding in your hands sixteen such journeys.

My own first Intrepid Journey lasted about twenty minutes. To this day it is one of the most profound of my life, as in many ways it set the scene for so much to come. It was in Nairobi and I was about twelve years old. My mother and I had travelled to Kenya to meet up with my elder brother who was working there. For some reason I was alone in the centre of the city and had to make my way back to the hotel a couple of kilometres away. Rather than get a taxi as I was told, I decided it would be more fun to walk. No sooner had I begun, than I found myself way out of my comfort zone. It was all so different from home. The relative security of the city degenerated as I walked into threatening squalor in the suburbs. There were people loitering aimlessly, looking at me and sizing me up and down. Thumping music came from minivans that seemed to carry half of Nairobi. Exotic, strange smelling food wafted out from street-side cafés. Rubbish littered the pathways that lined the muddy potholed streets. It was a challenge to my senses. A challenge that I had never experienced before. It was exciting, but also threatening. It was an Intrepid Journey and it left me hankering for more.

Since then I have been fortunate enough to experience a few of the Intrepid Journeys in this book – I have taken the hair-raising bus from Baguio to Sagada in the Philippines, the rattling train to Mandalay in Burma and a river boat along the Mekong in Laos. I have 'gone ape in Sumatra', 'taken the trunk road' in Thailand and battled my way down Highway One in Vietnam.

I am pleased to introduce this book, not for the fact that I can validate these tales, but because I can relate to them so well. They reflect my own attitude to travel – that it is the journey that is important, rather than the destination. It is the people and faces you meet along the way and the experiences you have, both good and bad, which constitute travelling. Ticking off a string of sights, no matter how impressive they might be, is never quite the same as an Intrepid Journey. Somehow sights do not capture your spirit, stir your imagination or touch your soul in the way an Intrepid Journey does.

So sit back and read on. Embrace the stories and atmosphere of Asia. But when you have finished reading, put the book down and think for a short while about taking the next step, creating your own Intrepid Journey.

As entertaining as this book may be, it is only a collection of someone else's stories. Intrepid Journeys are within us all – we just have to venture out of our comfort zone for a little while to see what happens. The results are not predictable, but when we return we will have discovered a little more about the world and a lot more about ourselves. We will be much richer for the experience.

Happy travelling!

Darrell Wade
Director, Intrepid Travel

Russia's Greatest Love Machine

by Ian Jackson

It started tentatively. We regarded each other nervously, neither had complete trust in the other. We knew, however, that this trust would have to be established as we would be bound together for the next three months. Our futures in Vietnam were inextricably linked and one's survival in the mountains and along Highway One depended on the other.

There were nervous outings along the bustling, noisy streets of Hanoi but over the next ten weeks the shyness and unfamiliarity were to be transformed into a blossoming love affair. My Russian beauty and I had great times and bad times. Times so bad I cursed like never before and threatened many times to leave her by the roadside when she stubbornly refused to budge, but come the next morning she was always there, ready and waiting for the day's adventures. Together we explored Vietnam and discovered ourselves and our limits.

Even the long journey into Saigon through gridlocked streets, trucks and buses belching foul diesel smoke at us while the fierce midday sun and humidity sapped our energy, was made bearable – if not enjoyable – because we were doing it together.

My 125cc Russian Minsk and I.

I was sitting at the Happy Café on Beijing Lu in Kunming with John, a thirty-one year old from Denver. We had left the Kunhu Hotel a few doors away and were whingeing about all things Chinese. There was a horrible feeling of *deja vu* about the morning. Yesterday we had stumbled out of the Kunhu hoping never to see the cold, grey concrete walls and resident cockroaches again . . . but here we were again.

Trying to catch the train to Hekou and the border to Vietnam we were stopped at the gate to the platform. Our tickets were inspected amid much muttering. We smiled blankly as more and more officials were called over and our tickets were passed around. It seemed like everybody at the station was going to have a look at them. Meanwhile, as people piled onto the train our chances of getting a seat looked remote. Finally a guard spoke: 'Chinese tickets'. They had finally cottoned on. We brandished our black market Chinese student cards, protesting that we came from a remote part of the Xinjiang province where everybody had blue eyes and a big nose, but we failed to convince. Voices were raised, a crowd gathered, and while we were trying to retrieve our tickets, we noticed the train slowly chugging away, heading towards Vietnam, escaping this crazy country.

The next day we were back at the train station, the only difference being that I was having internal eruptions that would have made Krakatau look like a hiccough. Not only had we had another night at the Kunhu, I had become intimate with the trough in the squat bog.

The tickets were in order. I was looking forward to Vietnam. The country was indelibly etched in my mind from countless war films and newspaper stories about Australia's involvement in the war. I had images of green patchwork quilt fields, men in combat fatigues and people on pushbikes.

What had happened to the people after the war? Was it a bastion of communist red tape as China had been? Were the people as bitter about the war as they were at home? Being Australian, would they be angry with me?

Russia's Greatest Love Machine

'That sounds like Neil', said John.

'Uh', I grunted and rolled over trying to catch a few more winks whilst telling myself that I did not really want to go to the toilet. John opened the window of our room in the guest house and stared down at everybody eating their breakfast.

'It is. Neil how yar going?'

Fifteen shocked faces looked up at a thin American grinning inanely down at them.

'When did you get in? We got here a few days ago. There's space up here if you haven't got a bed.'

Neil just waved, 'Hi John, is Jacko with you?' I lazily held my hand up and waved. The toilet was winning the battle of wills with my bladder. While John went to talk to Neil I climbed down the ladder to the ground floor and strolled through the kitchen. Squatting flat-footed, our hosts were preparing food on chopping boards on the floor as the cockroaches flitted about. I mumbled a hello as I weaved around them and the cat, and found the toilet.

I joined the guys: 'pho ga and ca phe. Cam on' (chicken noodle soup and coffee, thank you). John had that strange glint in his eye. I had seen it before and it usually meant some bizarre scheme had come to mind.

'Neil wants to buy a bike and ride to Saigon.'

'A bike? I'm not pedalling a bloody pushy from one end of the country to another.'

'A motorbike you twat', chimed Neil.

'A motorbike!! Out there? It's suicidal on those streets. Christ, just walking around is death-defying enough for me mate.'

We spent the next three days prowling around Hanoi looking for travellers who had ridden up from Saigon. Sitting over a cold 333 beer we were despondent. January was not the time to buy bikes and the thought of buses and trains the length of the country was not inviting. We pictured our trip around Vietnam as an Asian version of *Easy Rider*.

We heard them before we saw them. It was a different roar to the 'Honda Dreams' that prowled the city. Then they were there: two Minsks and a Czech Jawa. The riders looked tired, dirty and hardened. We waved them over. A couple of beers and some determined haggling

11

later the bikes were ours, pending a health check. Neil, a mechanic, gave them the once over and returned, hands covered in grease. Thumbs up. We arranged to meet them that night.

The next morning we were proud owners of emptier pockets, a motorbike, a wealth of information about where to go and stay, and hangovers big enough to have repelled the entire Viet Cong army at the DMZ. Now came the test. John and Neil were keen for a ride around town to get the feel of their bikes. It was the day before Tet (the Vietnamese New Year) and the city seemed even busier than normal as everyone went about their last minute chores before shutting the city down for four days of celebrations.

'Ah, guys, there's a small problem', I spluttered. 'I've never sat on a bike before, let alone tried to drive one.'

Suddenly this seemed very stupid.

'Look, here are the brakes, the accelerator, the clutch and you do this with your feet to change gears. This is neutral so you don't stall. Right, off you go then.'

'Cheers Neil, what a great teacher.'

I was sweating despite the fact it was cold. My hands were clammy and my stomach was churning. A crowd had gathered to watch three silly big noses with their motorbikes. Great. Here I was, twenty-eight years old, wondering where I could buy a set of training wheels, being watched by people who start riding bikes before they can walk. I am convinced some of them are born on the things.

Crunch, splutter. Crunch, splutter. Crunch, splutter. You bastard. Crunch, harder, crunch, crunch, crunch. Finally it sprang to life. Put it in first gear, ease out the clutch, slowly bring back the throttle. I stalled. Red-faced and with laughter ringing in my ears I started the bike again. It worked first time. Slowly roll along, wobble from side to side and gingerly lift both feet onto the pedals. I picked up speed and changed into second gear. The engine growled at me as I slowly got into gear. I can do this. Ahead of me a guy was sitting pillion on the back of a 'Honda Dream', arms outstretched and holding several panes of glass. I made a mental note to avoid this man.

For thirty minutes I rode the streets of Hanoi, gradually gaining

Russia's Greatest Love Machine

confidence. After a while I relaxed, started to look around me and stopped strangling the handle bars. School girls, three on a bike, whizzed past me, ducking in and out of the traffic and laughing at the ungainly Westerner. I did not care, the wind was in my hair, I was getting around Hanoi the way the locals do. I may not have been one of them but I felt part of them.

'You made it back, you've been gone so long we thought you'd already smashed the thing', said John.

'No worries. Get that map and let's have a beer.'

A new adventure was about to begin.

The packs were strapped onto the bikes, the maps had been studied and we said our goodbyes. The plan was to put as much distance between Hanoi and ourselves as we could on the first day and then take it from there. I gave Minsk a pat on the petrol tank, pointed her down Hang Quat Street and asked her to treat me kindly.

Getting out of Hanoi proved to be tougher than I had anticipated. Wheeling around Le Thai To Street and Hoan Kiem Lake, we crossed through the old quarter of Hanoi and out through the grimy industrial suburbs of the city. The road was packed with old blue Chinese trucks spewing smoke and soot over us. It was cold, and despite my thick down jacket, the wind ate into my bones. Weaving in and out of the traffic, trying to keep up with John and Neil without biting the dust took all my concentration. Suddenly the road opened up, the buildings became less frequent and rice paddies appeared on the side of the road. Highway One stretched into the distance and as the number of homes by the road dropped, the number of potholes increased. Some could be avoided by riding on the wrong side of the road. Ahead you could see the Vietnamese on their scooters weaving from one side of the road to the other. Occasionally my concentration lapsed and I bounced through the air as a pothole tried to throw me. I was amazed at how good the bastards were at jumping out and catching us by surprise.

Buses roared past, forcing us onto the dirty verge. Occasionally an old lumbering rust bucket of a bus that looked as if it was held together by string passed us. Rattling around, it would sway from one side of the road to the other in a vain attempt to bypass the potholes. Little Minsk

Intrepid Journeys

saw this as a chance to show her power. Inching up beside the bus, she would slowly crawl up to it. Heads would be glued to the windows, staring at the strange thing overtaking them. More heads would appear and the over-balanced bus would lurch towards us. Like a cork we shot past each time into clear space.

Minsk was thirsty and I was hungry so we stopped at a collection of rambling wooden shacks for lunch. I do not know what caused the greatest interest or laughter: the sight of three dirty big noses trying to order noodles or the two Minsks and the Jawa outside. When it was understood that we were going to Ho Chi Minh City the locals talked, pointed at the bikes and fell about laughing. We shrugged our shoulders. It was time to go. My arms were stiff from holding on to the bucking bronco that passed for a bike and it was a further hundred kilometres or so of playing chicken with buses and trucks before our planned stop for the night, Thanh Hoa.

The following morning Minsk was refreshed and patiently waiting for me. However, the previous day's battering at the hands of Highway One had taken its toll. Oh, how easily women play men for the fool. No amount of tinkering or cajoling would get her moving. The only sound of life was the odd splutter when I tried to kick-start her into action. However, after a push-start we were on our way to Vinh.

Vinh was bubbling over with celebrations for Tet. People were running around town, fire crackers were being exploded and cavalcades of young Vietnamese cruised up and down the main drag on motorbikes. We pulled in at a small place selling petrol and John and I rested while Neil pulled out a tool kit. After adjusting the chain Neil pulled the clutch and gearbox apart. Within minutes he was covered in oil and grease. A crowd gathered to watch and laugh as Neil hit, cursed and threatened to set fire to the Jawa.

'Neil, your lights are on mate.'

'What?' He reached up to turn them off. His key was gone.

'OK, give it back', he ordered, holding out an oily hand. He was greeted by innocent stares and grins.

'I'm bloody serious. Give me the key', he said, pointing at the bike and miming turning the key in the ignition. No response. Neil got

Russia's Greatest Love Machine

angrier and angrier.

'Have you got a spare?' I asked.

'No.'

Hoping they would get bored with their game of hide-the-key, Neil rebuilt the gear box and stormed off to a nearby noodle shack. A minute later he was back with several chopsticks. He whittled away at the end of one and jammed it in the starter, kick-started the bike and it spluttered before dying.

'Lets get out of here before you start another war', I suggested.

'Can't mate, the little bastard who turned the lights on has flattened the battery.'

It was only day three and we had covered about an inch on the map between Hanoi and Saigon. This could be a long trip.

When we finally headed off, the driving rain made riding difficult. The road was in a pitiful condition. Dodging potholes almost sent me sliding into the nearest rice paddy while riding through them sent painful jolts up my spine. We rode through Ben Thuy, Can Lac, Thuch Ha and Ha Tinh, Cam Xuyen, Quang Khe – the names and the kilometres clocking up.

After the Ky Anh Highway the road turned towards the sea and ran along the coast. I could smell the sea air and could hear and see the waves crashing onto the beach. Mother Nature was not in the best of moods. The wind lashed at my face while the driving rain stung my eyes.

Slowly climbing the Hoanh Son Mountains in the Deo Ngang Pass, Minsk was straining under the pressure, letting me know she was not happy. However, each time she threatened to stall some gentle cajoling or cursing did the trick. Close to the summit the clouds parted and the sun streamed through. As if the thought of warm sunlight on her aching body inspired her, Minsk kicked forward, found the peak and began the easy descent. For one of the first times I felt as if I was cruising. Rolling down the mountain, leaning left, leaning right, to guide her around the corners, all I needed was somewhere to put my feet up.

Dong Ha was a former command centre for the US marines and is still a strange frontier town, twenty-two kilometres from the Ben Hai River, and the old border between north and south Vietnam. The road into and through town was badly potholed. I was beginning to think Vietnam had a fetish for them. The other roads were rivers of mud after the recent heavy rain. Minsk was not happy and Jawa was suffering. We headed out to the Vin Moch tunnels, 2.8 kilometres of tunnels built on three levels. The maze of forks and weaving passageways are testament to the tenacity of the Vietnamese and their willingness to sacrifice everything to win the war. We took it easy in the driving rain on the way back from the tunnels. We were joking about the rain and our rally driving in the mud when we saw a group of Vietnamese drunkenly staggering down the road. They saw us and moved apart, leaving a gap for me to ride through. As I got closer they closed the gap and then created another one. I slowed and changed angle. They closed that gap and made a third space. I had no choice but to go for it.

As I passed them one jumped onto the handle bars, making me lose control of Minsk. The next thing I knew we were sliding on our side across the highway. I tried to lift my head up to keep it off the road and wondered if John was doing the same. It was strangely silent. All I could think of was the rice paddies and trees which were getting closer and closer.

There was no pain.

We slid to a stop.

'John, are you OK?'

'Yeah, what about you?'

'Fine, I think. Where is that little bastard? I'm going to kill him.'

I ran down the road to the Vietnamese guy who was lying in the road holding his ribs, and started screaming. His mates yelled at me.

'Cong An. Cong An.'

'Go and call the bloody police, see if I care.'

Heads had popped up from the rice paddies and people started running over to us. Where had they all come from? Suddenly the odds did not look healthy. Time to beat a hasty retreat. We walked over to poor Minsk and picked her up. The clutch cable had snapped. It was then that I realised how much my hand hurt. Three fingers on my right hand were bloody and already swollen. The little finger was at a crooked angle and I could see the bone on the knuckle joint. This was not good

Russia's Greatest Love Machine

– we were badly outnumbered, I had a stuffed hand and a bike that would work only in first gear. They continued to point and yell. We yelled back loudly and started Minsk. John rode into town while I sat on the back of Neil's bike, tenderly holding my hand.

Poor Minsk had seen better days but soon she was as good as new – well, as good as she was going to get – and ready for the next stage. I realised it was going to be impossible to ride her. I could not even bend three fingers on my right hand, let alone grip the accelerator. Riding was out of the question.

I would have to get a bus to Hue and wait for the guys. Having decided this came the hard part – seeing if we could get the bike on one of the tiny blue, yellow and red buses that looked as if it had come straight out of a Noddy story. At the bus station it was easy enough to organise a fare for me – Minsk was another thing. A friend started climbing on the roof of the bus, heaving her up. The two bus drivers were dancing and jumping around screaming. They tried to pull it down. The boys pushed it back up. Up, down, up, down, up, down and up again before Minsk was tied on to the roof. Poor old Minsk was strapped awkwardly to the roof with bags and several pigs. Very undignified. I hoped she would not take it out on me.

A deal was settled over a few beers. They would take me to Hue bus station where someone would take me on the back of his bike to the hostel while a friend rode Minsk from the station.

Somehow everything worked out. The driver spoke to two of his mates, pointed at me, pointed at Minsk still strapped to the roof and laughed. He then took me over to a little scooter and pointed to the back of the seat. His friend kick-started Minsk into action at the first attempt. Typical, and after all the love and care I had given her. Soon we were in traffic, floating effortlessly towards the centre of the ancient imperial city. After a couple of beers as a reward and much arguing over me attempting to pay them, they were off. Strangers but friends who will never be forgotten for their kindness.

Hue, the former home of the emperors, is traditionally Vietnam's cultural and religious home. With the Perfume River winding its way lazily through the city it is a beautiful spot. There is little to remind you that it was the site of the bloodiest battle of the 1968 Tet Offensive.

With only one hand working properly it was great to casually pedal my pushbike around town, taking in the beautiful pagodas and royal tombs. However, it was a strange sensation to have feeling in my rear end for twenty-four-hours-a-day again.

One of the popular traveller's hangouts in Hue is run by Lac, a deaf mute and his family. His daughters spoke English. Lac entertained the customers. When Lac discovered we were travelling through Vietnam on motorbikes he told us about his glory days before the war. He had been a stunt rider and showed us pictures and newspaper clippings of him pulling wheelies.

Lac had a mischievous side. At night he would sit with a map, point out towns and write down where we could get cheap beer and women. One night he decided he was going to come with us. He said he would sneak off without telling his daughters as they would attempt to stop him. He would ride to Saigon with us, taking us to all the beer joints and 'boom boom' places in south Vietnam. However, the night before we left he said he could not come as his daughters had suspected what he was up to and were angry. He did not want to make them sad. We laughed and shook his hand goodbye.

Halfway through the 106 kilometre journey to Danang, Minsk took revenge for being strapped to the roof of a bus and being cheated on during my affair with a pushbike in Hue. Her chain slipped and one of the sprockets broke. I could not get her out of first gear and she moaned and groaned along. Up ahead was the Hai Van Pass in the highest mountain range in Vietnam, a steep climb over the pass before the descent to the coast and Danang. The sun was beating down and merely sitting in the shade made us sweat. Minsk was not going to make it over the pass.

Several trucks pulled up for lunch. Bingo.

'Danang, anyone going to Danang?'

Three of them looked up and nodded vigorously. I pointed to Minsk and said 'Moto, bad', as I walked over and pretended to pick it up and throw it into the trees. The drivers laughed and squatted next to Minsk. They poked her, pulled some spanners out of the truck and fiddled around. Shaking their heads, they pointed at the engine and babbled away. Minsk was put in the back of the truck while I took a seat in the cabin. The three guys were a riot. Every time we passed young girls on motorbikes they would yell and whistle out of the window, asking me if I thought they would be good for 'boom boom'. Ahh, truck drivers.

The beautiful riverside town of Hoi An felt like home the minute we rode into town. The bustling market, the restaurants along the river and the nineteenth-century wooden buildings in narrow streets cried out at you to stay and soak up the atmosphere.

We took the dirt track out of town for five or six kilometres to the beach past shrimp farms, bamboo huts and lush, bright green paddy fields. It was a spectacular beach with small breaks washing up on the shore. We swam in the refreshing water and ate clams cooked over hot coals on the beach. Every afternoon school children would wheel their bikes and men would herd their cattle along the beach. It was a beautiful way to spend our days before riding back to town in the darkness.

One night we rowed across the river to an island to meet a skilled local painter. He used to play in a local band and he played and his wife sang traditional songs for us as we shared a bottle of whisky. After two weeks in Hoi An it was time to pack up and leave. We were looking forward to heading through the central highlands and to the change of scenery from Highway One. There were no buses where we were going so tourists were rare.

We thought Phuoc Son would be an easy 110 kilometre ride. We were wrong. Eight hours later we rolled into town, tired, dirty and sore. Soon after turning inland we left the tarmac and hit a stone road. These were not normal stones, they were boulders. If the back wheel hit a large enough one it skipped out, and I spent the first hour getting used to the bike jumping left or right without the slightest provocation.

The road wound its way through the mountains and breathtaking scenery. Lush fields gave way to forests and a winding river followed the road. Villages were built of spartan mud and thatch huts. The people were a mix of four ethnic groups – Bahnan, Jarai, Renago and Sedan. They stared at us unlike any others we had come across in Vietnam. Several times we stopped to swim in the river and relax in the rapids as

Intrepid Journeys

the cool, relaxing water swirled around us. Who needs buses?

Dac Lei was a friendly town where the locals used gas lamps to light their homes at night. At one noodle shop the Vietnamese owner told us he had been a paratrooper with the US forces during the war. A guy eating with us at the table wrote 'VC' on a piece of paper and the two began chatting. It was a strange feeling to be with two people who were once enemies but were now happy in one another's company.

Over another meal we met Mr Rin, a local man who teaches English. He took us to a Christian Church that was built a century ago. Their we met Rock and his brother. Their father was the chief of a village about one hour outside Kontum and their sister was getting married the following day. We were invited. When we arrived at the wedding the ceremony was in full swing. People were sitting around large jugs of *sitcong* – barley and wheat left to ferment for three months in a large jar covered with banana leaves and drunk through bamboo straws. We were expected to drink with each group in the village. We were also given shot glasses containing a clear, potent liquid. According to custom, every time we drank a glass we were given a small raw fish to carry around. There were loads of old men, stumbling bandy-legged around the village with a fistful of fish. Combined, both drinks were a wicked concoction that took their toll.

The next day we went back to the coast, to Pleiku, Phu Danh, the An Khe Pass, Bin Dinh, Qui Nhon, Song Cau and past isolated golden beaches and turquoise seas to Nha Trang. There was the usual bevy of vehicles and animals on the road. Sometimes it was difficult to work out who had the most road sense, the animals or the humans.

With her green hat, loud laugh and love of life local legend, Mama Hahn was easy to find. We had been told about her in China and were keen to try one of her boat trips out to the islands. Mama Hahn was not running her trips but she took us in as part of her extended family and invited us to dinner every night. Beneath the rough facade lay a tender, kind-hearted woman. She had just adopted a baby girl who had been dumped at the local market and who was proudly shown to us as if she was one of Mama Hahn's own.

There was nothing Mama Hahn loved more than feeding you before going out for a drink.

'Why you not eat?'

'I'm full, no more.'

'You must eat, you too skinny.'

'Me? Look at you, you're tiny.'

'I'm not skinny, I am thin boned.'

Just before we left, Mama Hahn got her boat up and running again and we had one of our most glorious days in Vietnam – and the best food by a mile. We did not want to leave but we had to get to Saigon via Phan Thiet where we planned to get the bikes looking their best for buyers. We set about the running repairs and were amazed to discover that every piece of the Jawa had been removed at some stage and that most parts of Minsk had been taken apart. It was amazing they had got this far. They had been pushed up and down the country so many times, all they wanted to do was lie down and die. But here we were refurbishing them so they could begin the journey all over again.

It seemed like every bus, truck, car and motorbike in the country was on the road into Saigon. The heat and belching petrol fumes from trucks was suffocating. Riding into the city I remembered what it had been like trying to navigate the streets of Hanoi. This was a much bigger, bustling city, yet riding around was infinitely easier. Nothing seemed to phase me. I just kept my hand on the horn and casually rode around any obstacle that happened to be thrown in my way.

Before we knew it we were in District 1 and the backpacker café strip. We were stared at by the Westerners this time, sitting with their ice cream or beer or spring rolls, with their clean clothes, scrubbed faces and pristine guidebooks. God knows what we must have looked like, covered in filth and cruising effortlessly in and out of the traffic with one hand on the horn. We stopped outside a café, climbed off the bikes and sat down.

'Where did you hire the bikes guys?'

'Hanoi. We bought them.'

'Cool man.'

People looked on in some strange kind of awe while all we wanted was a place to sleep . . .

Intrepid Journeys

Saigon was hot, damn hot, and after a week we were beginning to think we would never sell the bikes. We had placed notices at all the hostels and cafés but there were no takers. Neil and I were sitting in a café one day when two guys walked up, stating, 'We were told you guys had bikes for sale.'

'Yeah mate, whaddya wanna know?'

The deal was completed. Minsk sold for US$250.00 – the same price I had bought her for in Hanoi. I felt strangely empty inside. John and Neil were happily pointing out the places to stay, where to go and where not to go. Impulse made me say it: 'Mate, do you mind if I take her for one last ride around town?' 'Yeah, go for it. Smash it and I want my money back.' 'Here you go, hold on to it until I get back. Won't be long.'

I sat on Minsk and she started with the briefest touch. We rolled down Le Loi Boulevard, weaving in and out of the traffic. I turned the corner into Dong Khoi Street, saw a gap, twisted down the accelerator, clicked my foot rapidly through the gears and spurted past several 'Honda Dreams'. I had to hear that whine one last time. I rode around for about an hour. Cruising the streets of Saigon with the wind in my hair and without a care in the world, I felt a strange bond for the old bucket of nuts and bolts despite my repeated urges, throughout our journey, to blow her up or ditch her in a rice paddy.

I was tempted to head back to Hanoi. One last journey for the people I had met along the way – Mr Rin, Mama Hahn, the old villagers with their fists full of fish, the truck drivers and the countless people who helped patch up Minsk. She had induced the strangest feelings in me – incredible loneliness, deep anger and indescribable happiness. But it was time to let her go. I took her back.

As she rode off I watched her turn a corner and stall in the middle of the road.

That's my baby.

From Arms To Alms

by Juliet Coombe

The sun rose through the mist as the monks chanted, their bare feet shuffling through the dust. The first rays of sunlight turned their gowns golden. Just as civilisations change, Buddhism will remain. The saffron robes glistening like a beacon through the centuries of wartorn Laos. In time-honoured tradition, in peace as in war, the monks take to the streets of Luang Prabang, the former capital of Laos. Every morning the head abbot looks at the palm of his hand and when he sees his veins light up he pronounces that dawn has broken and that it is time to leave the temple and proceed along the main thoroughfare to gather offerings from the local people in old wooden alms bowls. Following in lines of up to one hundred or more, monks from each temple stop in turn to collect handfuls of sticky rice.

There are many ways to travel to Luang Prabang, a city described by many as an earthly paradise. It can be reached by a forty-minute flight from Vientiane, the capital of Laos, or by a five- to six-day boat journey along the meandering, enchanting Mekong River. For those on a budget, an increasingly popular option is over-landing it from Thailand, taking the sleeper train from Bangkok to Chiang Mai. I decided this option was the most romantic and would give me a real sense of the country and its remote hilltribes.

Arriving in Chiang Mai after a terrible overnight trip, I was not so sure of the wisdom of my choice. However, I quickly cheered up after a large noodle soup. Finding the main bus station was easy and I took the first one heading for the Thai/Laos border at Chiang Kong.

The immigration formalities at the northern border were extremely relaxed and friendly. In no time at all I had crossed over and boarded a motorised wooden boat, on which I was to travel downstream for two days. Sitting on the tin roof gave me an ideal vantage point to enjoy the spectacular Mekong scenery. The journey took me past forests, craggy stone cliffs, sandy shores and the homes of a variety of different hilltribes, many still wearing traditional dress. The children ran alongside the boats shouting 'Sabaai-dii' – hello in Lao – and were thrilled when the boat docked.

Most people stay overnight at Pakbeng, a dusty, rustic village with two basic hotels built around courtyards. It is a wonderful place where I had my first introduction to drinking *lao lao*, an alcoholic substance made from sticky rice, tasting not dissimilar to turps. Pakbeng has only one restaurant and one has to eat early, for at 9.00pm the tables are cleared and the room is transformed into a dance hall.

The owners played a combination of Lao folk and pop music, with one old man playing on a bamboo pipe and a set of gongs. As the tape crackled and started to blast out xylophonic music and twangy Lao singing, everyone joined together in three circles known as *lam wong* circle dancing. One person in the middle dances while couples circle past the central figure and a third tier is created by the rest of the crowd. Once the Lao people start to move to the rhythm of the music, they will accept no excuses from shy foreigners, as refusing to join in is taken as a direct and personal insult to their ancestors. The central dancer moves his or her hands like a snake charmer and, as I whirled around the circle, I found myself learning the delicate steps, my feet tapping in unison with the local girls as a pair of drums was brought out of the kitchen and played with wild abandon. Somehow, the Southeast Asian drum beat complemented the tape perfectly, creating harmony in the basic wooden room, which was now full of some hundred or more locals.

I found folk dancing quite spellbinding, providing a delightful way to get acquainted with the people of Pakbeng, who enjoy nothing better than a good old dance. 'In Laos, one's beauty is judged not by the face or the shapeliness of one's legs, but by the delicate intricate movement of hands', explained one woman, looking disapprovingly at the lack of movement in my hands. 'Can you weave?' she asked, and on discovering I could not, explained that my chances of marrying are unlikely. I tried to copy the lead dancer, but to no avail. Westerners amuse the locals no end with their large, clumsy, cumbersome movements, but after yet more *lao lao* no one cares. It is considered bad luck to refuse to down a jigger of *lao lao* in one and after a few rounds it did not seem quite so unpleasant. It was certainly a night I will never forget. Nor the following morning, when no amount of bottled water, headache tablets or sticky rice helped me to recover. Husbandless, I continued on my travels, enjoying the cool breeze of the Mekong.

As we chugged along, I smothered my face in sun cream, hiding the night's excesses behind dark glasses. The motorised boat's next port of call was the Pak Ou caves. It takes about five hours to reach the limestone cliff at the mouth of the Nam Ou River, unless you take the fast boat and are prepared to wear a motorbike helmet. The caves are easy to access up hand-cut steps and although some people dash to the top, I started with the lower cave, Tham Ting. It was filled with more than a thousand Buddha statues, some thick with bat droppings, spiders' webs and dirt dating back some four hundred years. Under one of the Buddhas was a jar with numbered sticks and a wooden box with white paper, covered with Lao writing. I was not sure of the purpose of it until a guide volunteered to tell me my fortune. He gave me the sticks, saying, 'Close your eyes and shake it until one pops out'. After a minute's deliberation and a great deal of shaking, number twenty-three jumped out. He picked up a piece of paper corresponding to the stick and

Intrepid Journeys

related nothing but bad news, and although I later noticed a lot of other temples had fortune-telling sticks, I never risked it again.

Further on up the cliff face is another cave, Tham Phum. This cave is much deeper and requires a torch to see the beautiful dragon carved into the arch of the cavern, with its scaly tail wrapping its way along the back wall. Water drips through a hole, creating an eerie echo in the cave, and after a frightened bird flew into my face, I decided it was time to leave. I made my way down the steep white steps and sailed on to the city of Luang Prabang, one of the latest places to be added to UNESCO'S World Heritage list.

Luang Prabang is extremely special, set amidst the mountains of northern Laos, on the junction of the Mekong and the Khan Rivers. It has become a major tourist attraction because of its thirty-two original temples and magnificent French provincial architecture. Few fail to be enthralled by its magical rain forest setting and if one only has a few days in the area, the places to visit must include the main royal temples (Wat Xieng Thong, Wat Visoun, Wat Sen, Wat Mai, Phousi Mount) and the Royal Palace where the royal family's quarters have been left untouched since their departure in 1975. Remember to dress suitably as I was refused entrance on the basis of my short sleeved t-shirt.

Templed out after three days, I decided to hire a motorbike in order to search for Henri Mouhot's tomb, the French archaeologist who discovered Angkor Wat. He died of malaria in 1861 and, like his discovery, his tomb was lost for one hundred years. Shortly after construction it was over-run by local vegetation and vanished as the rain forest ensnared it, only to be rediscovered accidentally by foreign aid staff in 1990.

The guide books tell you that the tomb can be reached up river some four kilometres from the cotton and silk hand-weaving village, Thai Lu. From there it is a further five hundred metres or so along the river bank, but its exact position is extremely vague.

It was a hot, dusty, windy day with an electric blue sky when I set off from Luang Prabang on my 'Honda Dream'. Locals walked past me carrying heavy bundles of wood in their arms and fishing nets slung over their backs. Women sat on their balconies weaving elaborate patterns from silk threads. Mounting the bike I set off for the weaving village, where I started asking for directions. Lots of fun was had trying out my basic Lao, combined with a range of interesting hand movements, that left the locals in stitches and me none the wiser. At the northern end of Thai Lu I met an old woman drying seaweed from the river. Her smile revealed a crooked batch of teeth stained red from years of indulging in beetlenut. I called out, 'Sabaai-dii', followed by, 'where is Mouhot's tomb?' Excited, she called her husband, who drew a simple map in the dirt track, pointing all the time at the river and mumbling, 'Mouhot, Mouhot, Mouhot'.

After many failed attempts to uncover the hidden tomb, I asked again at the next village. A shopkeeper informed me in perfect French, 'look out for an old wooden bench on the left hand side of the river, and descend a track, then walk up river from the bench'. Armed with the latest information I tried one last time to discover the resting place of the man who died some 137 years ago.

Down by the water's edge, at a section where the river runs fastest, lies Mouhot's burial chamber, a white marble tomb, simply engraved and yet majestic in its jungle setting. Listening to the water hitting the rocks and pouring over into the next loop of the river, I felt myself transported back to the Khmer ruins in Cambodia and back in time to a world of grandeur and dignity, a compelling and unrivalled period in history, offering universal appeal, past and present.

Here, in this enchanting and breathtakingly beautiful spot, I felt Henri Mouhot was merely sleeping and that his spirit would touch all who made the long trek to find him. Watching the fisherman pull in their nets, I decided to go for a quick swim before returning to town for a massage and a meal.

However long one spends in this romantic city, whether searching for one of Laos's million elephants or going for a swim in the emerald Kouangsy waterfall, one is always reluctant and sad to move on. Jumping on a plane at this stage is an excellent way to save time, avoid the risk of being waylaid by bandits or experiencing the frequent car breakdowns which can cause five to ten hour delays. My next destination was Thong Hai Hin or Stone Jar Plain, which is increasingly becoming one of Laos's most popular archaeological sites because of the mysterious bath tub sized jars scattered around the area in thirteen different groupings.

The mystery of the jars and their dramatic setting against the frontier town of Phonesavanh which was recently carved from the wilderness, could be passed off as a scene out of an Indiana Jones film. With the recent discovery of twelve sealed caves and ten more sites, interest can only continue to grow. Some say the jars are two thousand years old but many believe they are at least double that age. There is a constant archaeological debate about their possible uses but the general opinion is that they were made for ceremonial offerings to the dead. Of the many local theories, my favourite is that they are empties left over from some cosmic megalithic party thrown by the victorious king, Khun Jeuam, from South China.

Cut by hand out of sandstone rock and transported to the thirteen different sites by elephants, the jars seem to create a definite trail, connected together by guardian jars at the peak of each hill. If one examines an aerial map it is easy to see how all the sacred spots are linked together. Sadly, tourists are only allowed access to sites one, two and three, due to the huge numbers of unexploded bombs and land mines. Site one is called Ban Angnei and holds 298 jars of which the King Jar is the most famous, due to its vast size which overshadows the other smaller, rounder jars.

Further along the path is a hand-chiselled cave, where according to local myth the jars were created in a kiln using mud, water buffalo skin, sand, water, sugar cane and cement, fired together to create jars from six hundred kilograms to one tonne or more. The King Jar weighs an estimated seven tonnes and is quite awesome to stand beside. The cave, although dank, rank and filled with mosquitoes, did provide the perfect spot to view the bulk of the jars and escape the torrential rain. For the more adventurous, sites two and three have fewer jars but their picturesque hilltop setting, combined with the numerous water gardens that have filled the mouths of the jars, makes the additional twenty-eight kilometre drive well worth the effort.

Sadly not everyone chooses to visit the area to see these intriguing megalithic objects. Increasingly, people have become fascinated by the area because of its reputation as the most bombed place in the history of human warfare. As the Plain of Jars emerges as Southeast Asia's next tourist Shangri-La, there are now grave concerns about the best way to inform and not glamourise bombs and war scrap – particularly in the Xieng Khouang province, where huge bomb craters are scattered across the countryside. It was only as I flew in on a fifteen-seater plane that the true obscenity of this nine-year bombing campaign sunk in. We circled over huge sections of land which had quite literally been flattened with an estimated six to eight million bombs during the height of the Vietnam war. As far as the eye could see were huge brown sections of infertile land where ordnance had ripped massive sections out of paddy fields and mountains. Despite the war having finished twenty-five years ago, nothing will grow in these areas and even now, one person dies every other day from contact with ordnance. To many the war is not over, and with 11,600 deaths since it ended in 1973, the Laos people are extremely angry. 'We lost members of our families during the Indo-China war. We want to know where they are and we want to give them proper burials. The Americans spend millions looking for MIA's (American soldiers missing in action), but not one penny is spent on clearing up the ordnance that continues to cost us members of our families', explained a local headman.

Phonesavanh is built in an area still covered with live ordnance, so it is important not to take risks. In the week I was there they found a five hundred pound bomb outside the main hospital and sixteen bomblets on the road leading from the airport into town. With increasing pressure to enlarge the town and with the growing influx of tourists, tragedies are likely to become even more common. Since the jars were re-opened to the public in 1991, travellers visiting the site have increased from a handful to over four thousand this year.

Continuing my tour of the war-torn region, I visited the old capital of the Xieng Khouang province which is badly bombed, leaving only a rather damaged seated Buddha. It is only worth a visit if one has plenty of time. Many people go to the Bannasala Hmong village after visiting the Sunday market at Bannong Phet. The market requires a 5.00am start and is well worth visiting to see rats, cats, squirrels and bats being sold for consumption. Sunflower seeds lie drying in the sun while Hmong women with children wrapped in their baby carriers haggle over cones of lava and delicate green birds.

Returning to Phonesavanh I stopped at one of the many 'bomb villages', Bannasala. Everything from the grain stores balanced on stilts to fenceposts, animal troughs, boats and boxes to grow spring onions in, are made from bomb remains. A few hours away from Bannasala is one of the saddest sites, the Tam Phiu cave, where 365 people took refuge in March 1968 and were consequently killed by an American rocket. All that remains is a skull set on a twisted metal pole where people continue to leave wreaths of flowers in remembrance.

Flying on to Vientiane, it is strange after days of roughing it to suddenly be able to browse in one of the Raintrees chain of bookshops or to enjoy freshly-baked cakes at the Swedish or Canadian bakery by the Namphou Fountain in the town centre which is a buzz of cultural activity, commerce and administration.

As soon as I left the cosmopolitan centre I travelled through colonnades of beautiful banana and papaya trees, in search of a massage and herbal sauna at Wat So Pa Luang. Tuk-tuks act as transport to and from the forest temple, bouncing along the potholed roads. The Wat sauna treatment is made up of thirty-two herbs mixed into a boiling cauldron. The nuns prepare the concoction while teenage boys perform hourly massages which promise to eradicate all the aches and pains of the intrepid traveller.

For those interested in a day trip, explore Buddha Park off Thanon Tha Deua. The site is like a bizarre theme park, the most compelling object being the human head at the entrance which has three levels representing heaven, hell and earth. It is well worth going inside as the rooms are full of extraordinary sculptures and as I made my way up the spiral staircase, I had constantly changing views of the reclining

Buddha, Shiva and Vishnu statues before a magical view of the patchwork paddy fields that have remained unchanged by time.

After this memorable experience I was prepared for anything, even hiring a bicycle and seeing what Vientiane has to offer, starting with That Luang, Laos's most important national monument. After getting embroiled in a local festival, I cycled on to Wat Sisaket, Hor Prakeo, Wat Simuang, Anou Savaly, the Revolutionary Museum and the morning markets (open all day!), where one can purchase ancient and modern silk weavings. Laos has a rich tradition in textiles but sadly much has been lost. There are two women worth seeking out, a local Lao named Chanthorn Thattanakham and an American ex-pat, Carol Cassidy. The former can be found on the first floor of the morning market or just off Chinaimo Road, Ban Suanmone, Sisattanak District. Her home is an Aladdin's cave of antique weavings and she is one of the few people who recognises the importance of collecting old Laos textiles from the native villages.

Carol Cassidy has a showroom where one can watch the weaving in progress. Carol, as I discovered, is the Jim Thompson of Laos. She is not only reviving the country's rich textile history but can explain the mythical creatures, folk lore and rationale behind the colours and stitches used in the weavings. For centuries the Lao and other ethnic groups in the region have woven beautiful textiles. Historically, these fabrics served utilitarian purposes. Women from Champassak to Luang Prabang, from Sarravan to Sam Neua, wove ornate garments characterised by their individual creative expression. Thus began the diverse textile culture for which Laos is held in such high esteem. Sadly, due to war and changing economic circumstances, the ability to weave wonders slowly broke down and almost disappeared, but thanks to Carol Cassidy, the enthusiasm of the local women and growing international interest, traditional silk weaving has had a revival.

As I sat on Carol's gate watching a group of girls boiling silk, bobbins whirling, looms ticking away, a ballet of legs and arms transforming yarn into treasures, a group of monks passed by clasping their wooden bowls filled to overflowing with rice and other delicacies.

They walked in time to the clicking looms and their robes blew in the breeze, changing colours as the sun set. I wondered, as they disappeared into the dusk, how Laos would cope with the onslaught of the commercial world.

The Spirit Of The Naga

by Elliot Daniel

As I lay in my bed staring at the ceiling, another hot and steamy tropical Asian night enveloped me. The monotonous drone of the fan cut through the sticky air and sent me into a trance. Sleep came to me fitfully. From the dark sea of my deep unconsciousness there appeared a running and swimming twenty-foot dragon. It was an evolved and voracious hunter which scented its prey with a long, pink, forked tongue that flicked over the ground like a flame. I awoke suddenly and knew where I must go.

We began the adventure of a lifetime. My three friends and I were going trekking in the north-eastern highlands of Thailand, the Chiang Rai province. We went in search of the indigenous hilltribe people and the secrets the mountains had long contained.

Our first morning began perfectly. We met our guide Ut, who was a strong, wiry, forty-two year old northern Thai. He was charming, knowledgeable and his passion for the hilltribe people was infectious. Our trek began at the Mae Kok River as we were journeying by longtail boat into the mountains. As I lay back in the boat, with the wind in my hair and the spray cooling my hot body, a sense of serenity enveloped me. The pressures of life in the West seemed a world away. As we travelled up the river, Ut defined the tribes to which the children who fished along the rivers banks belonged. He also explained that the adjacent rice fields provided most of the lifetime livelihood for every man, woman and child in every village.

These indigenous peoples of northern Thailand are not actually native to Thailand. They originated further to the north and northwest, in the mountains of northern and south-western China, and in Tibet. They migrated slowly southwards over many centuries, first reaching Thailand in the eighteenth century. However, this century has seen the largest influx of peoples into the kingdom, as they have fled warfare and political instability in neighbouring lands. There are now some half-a-million indigenous hilltribe people living in the northern Thailand, the six principal groups being the Hmong, Karen, Akha, Lahu, Yao and Lisu, all of which represent ninety-five per cent of the country's population. Each group is unique, possessing its own distinct history, language and culture. They all, however, share one common way of life: all are farmers living in small agricultural communities which deeply revere the family social unit and the daily relevance of the surrounding spirit world.

The intoxicating effect of the thumping engine, the water lapping at the side of the boat, Ut's rhythmic voice and the tropical heat sent me into an enchanting daydream, where I joined that curious league of explorers who have risked life and limb in order to discover the sources of rivers, the profiles of mountains and the secrets of forbidden cities. I awoke suddenly, as the boat jolted to a halt on the banks of the river. 'Lunch time', Ut yelled over the drone of the engine. 'Hit the water and go for a swim but stay close to the bank. The river's very strong at this time of the year.' Within seconds we were in the cool, refreshing water. A set of rapids further upstream suddenly caught my attention and I decided it was time for some adventure. I walked along the bank for about a kilometre away from the others, as I marvelled at the lushness of

The Spirit of the Naga

the jungle and the vital role that river valleys play in providing life for man and creature.

Recklessly, I dived in and swam to the centre of the river above the rapids. The spray of the white water loomed closer and closer and time stopped momentarily. Suddenly, the river grabbed me. I took a huge breath and closed my eyes as it tossed me, spun me and spat me out. My heart thumping, I turned for the shore but my strokes were in vain as the relentless pull of the current continued to force me downstream. I struggled harder but to no avail. Panic seized me. I was heading for a larger set of rapids with protruding logs and debris. The rapids were a huge set of jaws waiting to swallow me. I was frantic and feared for my life, as, no matter how hard I swam, nothing happened. The river had me in its grip and would not let go. I was totally exhausted and my arms and legs were useless. My life flashed before me and I longed to give in. I closed my eyes and succumbed to the spirit of Naga.

I returned to consciousness on the bank, coughing and spluttering. Gradually, familiar faces and the sound of voices began to penetrate my numb brain. My companions had witnessed the entire event and had raced along the bank to help me, as they readily understood the life-threatening situation. They marvelled that the river had sucked my lifeless body into the vortex of a small whirlpool before tossing me out onto the bank of the river. Ut, who had been standing over me the whole time, began speaking in a soothing voice. To this day I do not remember all that he said but his words calmed me instantly. I can remember his final words, 'we are changing our trekking course slightly, I have someone very special for you to meet. When you are ready we will go'. I lay back, as secure as a child, as the sun's rays bathed me in their warmth. As two egrets soared into my vision I realised I had been given another chance to live and grow. I had learnt a lesson from this river and was truly awed by nature's pitiless power.

As we left the river for the mountains, Ut explained that our new course would take us to a remote Akha village four hours away. These people were refugees from Burma and had fled the brutal rule of the military junta, the SPDC (State Peace and Development Council). We climbed for a long time. Gradually, the paths became steeper and harder and my knees began to buckle under the strain. After two hours we stopped to rest. The day was extremely hot and mosquitoes continuously pestered us. The mountains loomed before us, as far as the eye could see. The light filtered through the lush jungle, dark green in the sun and blue in the shadows. We glimpsed a cluster of fifteen bamboo huts perched atop the mountains and I had my first sight of an Akha woman.

She wore traditional dress with her majestic headpiece a festoon of silver balls of all sizes, with buttons and old silver coins from Burma, India, French Indochina and Britain, colourful red and white beads, furs, feathered tassels and seeds from the jungle. Her clothes were made from home-spun cotton, dyed in indigo. Ut explained that it is the Akha custom for the male to buy the head dress for his future wife (some are worth thousands of American dollars) and that once she puts it on, she has to wear it for the rest of her life.

We wandered into the village amidst gawping eyes, faces that watched us from smoke-blackened interiors, howling dogs, screeching chickens and grunting pigs. It appeared as though everyone here was as fascinated by us as we were by them. After removing our shoes according to custom, we were ushered up to the village headman's balcony. While he and Ut spoke we received cups of refreshing, hot, bitter green tea. The shade of the verandah provided a cool respite from the heat of the day and we welcomed it wholeheartedly. After a while, Ut left the headman and came over to me, saying, 'do you want to meet that special person I told you about?'

We were welcomed into the village clairvoyant's house by Me-do, one of her four daughters. It was a traditional Akha home, made of bamboo and wood, complete with large, open verandah and a low sloping grass roof. The interior was dark, gloomy and fragrant with wood smoke. Beams of sunlight pierced the woven bamboo walls and together with the open doorway, provided the only source of light. A thin bamboo partition divided the interior into two main sections – one for the men and one for the women. My companions sat around the fire

The Spirit of the Naga

and took tea while I sat in front of the ancestral altar. Ut explained that I must sit with my legs facing away from the altar to show respect, as the feet are the most unholy part of the body.

I gazed at a frail woman who must have been over ninety. Her face and skin resembled craters from a barren, parched landscape. Slowly, she gently took my hand, softly chanting and blowing streams of breath onto my open palm, as she delicately traced its creases with her index finger. Her chanting gradually increased in volume and intensity as her hand shifted from mine, to the air, and then back again. No longer was she frail and weak, she became an all powerful entity of high-pitched screeching and frenetic energy.

Suddenly she spoke. Her divinations were interpreted by her daughter, which Ut then translated into English. She decreed that I would travel the earth for many years and that great fortune would be mine one day. Her daughter then paused, seemingly unsure of what to say next. Ut translated: 'You must be very careful of water. You have already been tested by the Naga of the river and you will be tested twice more'. An uncomfortable silence gripped the room. I was urged to stand and leave as the session was over. In traditional custom, I left enough baht for the price of a chicken, as one would be slaughtered to appease the spirits. I walked gingerly out into the afternoon sun, feeling as if I were floating, with her words ringing in my head . . . 'Be very careful of water . . . tested twice more'. How could she have known of my near drowning? No one had told her of my brush with death. Her words still haunt me.

Soon, we left the Akha village, heading for a Red Lahu village two hours away, where we would spend the night. As we walked, Ut explained that the indigenous people have a great fear of, and respect for, the spirits of water. Legend says that at certain times of the year the rivers are hungry and the Naga of the river must take someone's life so that the rains will come and the crops will prosper.

The sun was setting as we arrived at the village bathed in a golden glow. Thirty-two families have lived here for over twenty years. There were huge sighs of relief as we stopped to rest, allowing our weary bodies flop to the ground. We were spending the night at Ja Toe's house. He was the village headman, forty-two years old and with five children. The Lahu are famed as skilled hunters and the scrub pheasant that Ja Toe was proudly showing Ut was destined for the large pot that sat before us on a crackling fire. By the glow of homemade paraffin lamps, the women prepared the meal. Pieces of pork fat were torn from a row of meat hanging from the roof and then fried in a wok on the fire. In another pan huge handfuls of vegetables simmered with garlic and chillis. As the chillis hit the sizzling wok the fumes exploded, causing my eyes to water profusely. All the vegetables were fresh from the forest and included baby aubergines, fern tips, wild mushrooms and bamboo shoots. When these were removed, on went a wok full of rice cakes. Ja Toe returned with the plucked and naked pheasant, which was cut into pieces, and then thrown into the pot, feet and all.

The younger children were then called into the house and we sat in a circle to eat our meal. The family watched with pleasure as we hungrily scooped food into our mouths. It was truly delicious, albeit a touch spicy and was washed down with *lao kaew*, a lethal, homemade concoction of rice whisky. The effect of the whisky, after the events of the day and the reality of being perched on top of a mountain in the middle of nowhere, had my head spinning. We received large handfuls of freshly grown tobacco which was passed around in a huge bamboo pipe. One of the headman's sons then produced a musical instrument resembling a crude banjo. It was made of wood, had three wire strings running its length and fastened to pegs at the neck. He played a melancholy, mournful song that hung suspended in the smoky room. This hypnotic sound sent me drifting into another world. I was in total bliss.

It was the piercing, high-pitched shrill of a rooster that shook me from my dream. I thought roosters only crowed in the morning. This is not the case in the mountains of Thailand. Here they scream whenever they want, along with the pigs and the dogs. Through the crackling fire I saw Ut and Ja Toe chatting, and I was invited to listen. Ja Toe explained how the people of his village do not feel secure, as they have neither rights of citizenship nor legal rights of ownership to their land. His community has only enough land to feed itself, and the people fear clearing more land nearby as it is in a protected forest area of the Royal Forestry Department. Ja Toe had been told by other Lahu communities of how their men had been arrested for clearing similar land. He also spoke of education, explaining that although the village houses an elementary school in the village, the children cannot formally graduate or attend post-elementary schools. It is issues like these that the indigenous people face every day, in addition to their daily struggle to survive.

That afternoon I noticed that only a few people wore traditional costume, while the rest wore T-shirts and tracksuit pants. I realised that this village was going the way of so many other formerly remote hilltribe villages in northern Thailand and, indeed, the way of so many thousands of similar communities the world over. The unbridled force of the outside world is reaching out to suffocate the unique qualities on which a minority culture bases so much of its identity. In their rush to modernise their economies, the countries of Southeast Asia and especially Thailand are becoming increasingly drawn into the global capitalist economic order.

I awoke the next morning to those same roosters which slept directly under the hut. After a delicious breakfast of fried rice, we quickly packed our belongings as we had a seven-hour walk ahead of us. It was painful leaving Ja Toe, his family and the warmth of their home as they had offered us so much of themselves. After an hour's walk, I was covered in sweat and realised how tough and hardy these mountain dwellers are. Life is a constant struggle, both with the elements and with the onslaught of rapid change. We ascended and descended mountains, crossed river valleys and followed ridges along escarpments affording breathtaking views of mountainous, dense green jungle. The clear air exhilarated me. There is something magical about being deeply immersed in nature: life slows down and thoughts clarify as one is stripped of the stresses and time constraints dictated by life in the West. Walking through these mountains is a most rewarding way to experience their charm and to rejuvenate the spirit.

Intrepid Journeys

Late in the afternoon we arrived, exhausted and filthy at a small Akha village. Ut directed us to the communal tank where we could wash, much to the delight of the giggling onlookers. Daily washing is a huge social activity in the village. Children play gaily as they splash each other and they took great pleasure in teasing and splashing us. The Akhas are individually shy but in a group the women are very communicative and joined in the frolics. So, with bio-degradable soap in hand we dodged the mischievous children and dived into the mayhem. Rachelle and Antonette, my two companions, had to wear sarongs while they bathed, as this is the acceptable mode of dress for women. A pair of shorts sufficed for us men.

Clean and refreshed, we returned to our host, Apollo's, house. After another delicious meal, people began slowly wandering off to bed. Suddenly, a faint and distant drumbeat accompanied by an eerie wailing, caught my attention. I wondered if I was imagining these sounds and asked Ut. He spoke to Apollo, who paused, thought for a few seconds, then produced a huge grin, showing betel-blackened teeth. His hands gestured that we should go.

As we ventured into the blackness of night, the resonating boom drew us to one of the larger village houses, which I learned belonged to the shaman. As we entered the doorway I was not prepared for what I saw. At the front of the house, eight men and women danced in a circle. They followed an old man playing a large piped instrument whose melody was both haunting and enchanting. Behind him, a man was beating a huge drum, strapped to his body. In unison, all the dancers pounded their feet and spun and whirled to the beat of the drum. The entire house shook. As my eyes adjusted to the dimly-lit interior, I observed that along the walls people were resting, smoking and chatting quietly. At the back of the room on a raised platform sat the shaman, holding a ten year old boy in his lap. The shaman's eyes were closed as he chanted. Alongside him sat the boy's father, also chanting. Surrounding the two men were clay holders that covered small paraffin lamps and sent flickers of light dancing across the men's faces. We joined those sitting along the sides of the house and I gazed, frightened and fascinated. Ut explained that the young boy had fallen ill and that this ritual would exorcise the bad spirits from his body. The ritual had begun, earlier that day, with the sacrifice of a pig, in order to appease the spirits and would continue long into the night.

I slept heavily, in complete awe of the lifestyle of the indigenous people of northern Thailand. I realised that these people moved through life slowly and steadily, expecting nothing more than the cycles of the day, the seasons and their lives, here and after death. What a contrast to life in the West where we live in frantic little boxes. Here there was work, pleasure, day, night, where I am now and where I will be when I die.

Later, we left the village and made our way back down to the Mae Kok River. Apollo and his friend were joining us in order to finish the construction of bamboo rafts used for transporting supplies to their village up the river. As the sun reached its zenith, we arrived at the river. On the ground lay huge bamboo logs that would form the base of the raft. The men tied the logs together with binding, also crafted from bamboo. Watching them work was enlightening, as within an hour they had completed three rafts. These were skilled craftsmen who could fix or make virtually anything without destroying the natural environment.

With a splash our rafts hit the water and we were off. Ut and the two Akha men went first, followed by Antonette, Ryan and then Rachelle and myself. The rafts floated perfectly. As we punted down the river with long bamboo poles we revelled in the glorious day and the tranquillity of the river. Successfully steering the rafts resembles rally car driving, as you point the nose of the raft into the apex of the corner and then let the back slide out and around. After a few attempts we became confident and our tension subsided. Like children, we began to play, splashing each other with water.

As we approached a right hand bend in the river, water was crashing violently against an enormous rock. We slowed down to give each other space to navigate this section. Ut's raft went through, no problem. From behind, I could see that Antonette and Ryan had taken the corner too wide and were heading straight for the rock. It all happened within few seconds. Their raft smashed against the rock and sent them flying into

Intrepid Journeys

the air. As I had been oblivious to where Rachelle and I were going, our raft also went wide. As it hit the fast water our speed increased following a collision course with the other raft.

Then I glimpsed Antonette under the water and as she surfaced for her first breath of air, I realised that our raft would smash against the other, crushing her head. I screamed at Rachelle to jump off our raft as I leaned forwards, pushing Antonette's head back under the water, out of the raft's path, but in danger of drowning. I screamed at Ryan to grab her, and somehow, amidst the panic, confusion and deafening roar of the white water, we snapped into rescue mode. Ryan spotted her first. She was trapped under the lead raft. Ryan and I both dived in and managed to pull her from beneath the raft, up to the surface. She was safe.

Later, as we all sat on the side of the bank, soaked and shivering from the ordeal, those words kept running through my mind ' . . . be careful of water . . . tested twice more'. Was that my second time or was it Antonette's first? I yearned to see the clairvoyant again.

Those days have changed my life forever. I have glimpsed some of the mystery and magic of the mountains and the indigenous people. I have been tested by the spirit of Naga and have not been found wanting. While I remain in awe of the power of Naga, I am not afraid. I believe that nature and Naga combined to test me and then to enlighten me. I am humbler and, I hope, stronger. I will return.

Going Ape In Sumatra

Mike Gerrard

It began, as many a good adventure does, with a car chase. This was a race against time, although anyone who has ever seen a Sumatran drive will know that you do not want to be with them when they are in a hurry. Not for nothing are there smashed cars on concrete blocks displayed at the side of the road as a warning to other drivers. I did not know this at the time, as I had just stepped out of the airport; nor did I know that I was about to spend sixteen hours in a Sumatran taxi.

The trip had been planned for months but what had not been part of the well thought out organisation was the fires that raged through Sumatra in the summer of 1997. The trip was put back and back again but eventually in October it was given the go-ahead. Intrepid's Sumatran tour was to resume. The airports were re-opening and life was returning to normal.

Well, almost. I got to Kuala Lumpur to find my next-day connecting flight to Padang and the start of the tour cancelled. It was Saturday afternoon, most airline offices were closed and I had to be in Padang the next day as the tour was starting first thing Monday morning, presumably with or without me. Garuda in Jakarta informed me that I could fly through Jakarta to Padang, and they even offered to take over my Air Malaysia ticket as long as I paid the balance. I duly turned up at the Air Malaysia desk the next morning to re-route to find that they had booked me on a later flight to Padang, via Medan. The flight I was supposed to have taken had been cancelled but this later one was still going. Perfect.

I sat at the airport for five hours, flew to Medan, had an hour to walk to the adjacent domestic terminal, only to discover that the connecting flight had been cancelled. The airport was closed. Terrific. I later found out that the airport at Padang had, in fact, been open all day, and my fellow travellers on the tour had flown in on the aforementioned Garuda flight from Jakarta. Thank you, Air Malaysia.

So here I was on the wrong side of an island the size of California, with a possibility of another flight the next morning – but no guarantees. The bus would take twenty-four hours, by which time the tour would have left. It was ninety degrees fahrenheit and humid. I was still jet-lagged from the flight from England to Kuala Lumpur. I also hate being at airports when as a stranger in a strange land you are yet unsure and, hence, prey to every scam. Wonderful.

I phoned the contact number for the hotel but the tour leader had not arrived either. What to do? How much was a taxi? About US$140.00. How long would it take to drive to Padang? About sixteen hours. Deduct the cost of a night in Medan and then a two-hour taxi ride, anyway, from Padang airport to the tour starting point at Bukittinggi, and the taxi seemed the only option. I would be doing the entire tour in reverse, in less than a day, in order to get to the start and then spend two weeks getting back to Medan.

'Good car', the taxi driver said and then added, 'we don't go in this car, get you better car, air conditioned, good driver'. Was this where the fairness and welcoming nature of airport taxi drivers, renowned the world over, somehow went adrift? He drove me through the back streets

Going Ape in Sumatra

of Medan and switched me to a transit van. 'Air-conditioned', he said. I met my driver, Amir, and paid half the fare in advance. 'Pay rest to Amir in Bukittinggi', the first driver said, pocketing the wedge.

We set off. I was sweat-soaked already. 'Air-conditioning broken', said Amir. He smiled and pointed to himself. 'Amir', he said, then pointed to me. 'Mike', I explained. We shook hands. I had rather he had kept hold of the steering wheel but maybe I was just being fussy.

Amir has five children, I discovered, but that was about the extent of our communication. I tried to find out the names of his children, pointing at me and saying, 'Mike', and at him and saying, 'Amir', and then asking, 'baby?' but he just nodded, smiled and said, 'Baby, yes'. After five minutes of nodding and confusion, Amir then surprised me by saying suddenly: 'Bukkittinggi, beautiful panorama!'

It was Sunday afternoon and there were roadside concerts at several of the villages we passed through, using sound systems that would make a Jamaican jealous. At one, a lady in a yellow and black dress was standing at the microphone, with an Asian wail, backed by a Yamaha. The landscape was lush and I started to relax.

Boys with red flags were waving down the traffic and there was a small barrier across the road but they were only collecting for some cause with a few buckets. Amir tossed them some coins. It was the first time I had seen this roadside collecting, apparently common in Indonesia. We passed rice paddies where water buffalo wade.

A convoy of bikers, all wearing turquoise and white blousons passed us in the opposite direction. A police escort led the endless procession; up to half-an-hour later stragglers were still passing us. I asked Amir what it all about

'Apti-bedi', he replied.

'Apti-bedi?' I repeated.

'Yes', and began singing, 'Apti-bedi to you, apti-bedi to you . . . '

Quite what the bikes and turquoise blousons have to do with a birthday I did not know – nor did I ever find out.

In front of one house a boy was practicing his judo – it seems he was

Intrepid Journeys

a green belt. Every fifty yards or so, red and black Guinness signs stood out against the vivid green fields. We passed a sign for a garage which states: 'Petrol, oil, water, pispot'. Did it mean what I thought it meant?

We passed by forest after forest of palm trees, grown for the palm-nut oil. Under the trees people were selling bottles of juice and picnicking. I could almost have been in England.

We drove by rubber trees, thin trees all bent in the same direction in a wind-induced wave – just as if they were made of rubber. For mile after mile they swayed, row after row receding into the distance. Ten minutes later we were still driving past these rubber plantations, blue or white plastic cups strapped to the trees to collect the sap. They probably need so much rubber due to the way they burn it when they drive.

On a white stone block, with a silver skull painted on the side, was a crashed car, a warning to other drivers but a warning that is obviously ignored as Sumatran drivers are crazy. I realised that my life was in the hands of a complete stranger but Amir, in fact, proved to be a relatively safe driver . . . it was just the madmen coming the other way playing chicken in the middle of the road that had me worried.

One village was almost flooded away after recent rain, yet none of the villages on either side of it seemed affected. Yards were under brown water and children splashed one another while some adults sat glumly on chairs in waterlogged doorways, their feet in the water.

There were piles of coconuts for sale by the roadside, as well as some red fruit I did not recognise, huge plums, prickly jackfruit and the dreaded durian fruit – the fruit that smells so bad hotels ban it from their premises.

We stopped to buy water – two large bottles came to a few pence. Amir bought some cigarettes but insisted on paying for these separately, allowing me to buy only the water. I realised I was with a decent man.

The road started to rise and twist a little and for the first time we were looking down, onto a small wood. We passed a tramp wearing only ragged trousers, his skin a deep brown, wobbling drunkenly along the grassy verge – not very wise given the state of the driving.

Going Ape in Sumatra

Here they drive on the left – well, most of them do – but use the right hand indicator constantly. Sometimes the indicator seems to state that it is safe to overtake, at other times it seems to convey the notion that they themselves are about to overtake what is in front of them. Sometimes even – but not very often – it means that they are actually about to turn right. On occasion oncoming drivers use it – are they saying 'hello' or 'get out of the way'? Does the first one to switch his indicator on have right of way down the middle of the road?

We passed a small fairground in which there was a round multi-coloured wooden structure, a wall of death booth, such as I have not seen since I was a child. I was surprised they need it, given the way they drive on the roads, where every wall is a wall of death.

The sun began its descent, painting the sky pink behind the palm tree silhouettes. At 7.00pm we stopped in Prapat for supper. I could have had fried frogs and chips but I settled, instead, for braised sliced beef and ginger while Amir had a variation of a biryani, and together with my beer and his soft drink the meal came to the equivalent of about US$6.00. I went to a telephone office to try to make contact with the tour leader, to let him know I was on the way, and on locating him, was pleased to discover an affable American. I explained I was going to take a taxi from Medan to Bukittinggi. 'You're doing *what*?' he asked.

'Well', I said, 'it is an adventure holiday. Mine's just started early'.

'Wow, crazy man', he laughed, and I know we were going to get on fine.

Sometime after that the journey, quite literally, became a blur, as I had to remove my contact lenses in order to have a sleep on the back seat. We reached the Benteng Hotel in Bukkittinggi at about 5.45am and I paid Amir the balance of the fare as well as rewarding him with a very generous tip. We shook hands and I headed to my room for a shower.

Bukittinggi means 'High Hill' – there are a lot of Bukits in Sumatra and this one is nearly three thousand feet up in the Minang highlands. It is a compact town surrounded by green mountains, reminiscent of Indian hill stations and just as popular with locals and tourists for its cool climate on this island that straddles the equator.

At the introductory meeting, which I made with a sigh of relief, I took to the tour leader for his sense of humour, when he said: 'There's one major rule on our trips, and that's that you're not allowed to die. It creates too much paperwork'.

The Benteng Hotel had its own rules too: 'Clients who leave the hotel, should be decently dressed. Clients are not allowed to carry animals, fruits, that give off a terrible smell in room. Married couple who will stay at hotel, should show the marriage certificate'.

Decently dressed and hopefully not smelling too terribly, I explored the town, heading straight for the Pasar Atas central market, one of the biggest in the region. I spent an hour getting lost, finding myself again and then discovering whole sections I had never seen before. Some stalls were sinking beneath bananas, others were devoted to coconuts: 'You have coconuts in England?' a stall owner asked me. When I said we do not grow them, he was puzzled and asked why not. Nor, sadly, do we grow rambutans, passion fruit, mangosteens, papaya or any of the other rainbow fruit piled on the stalls, tempting both my taste buds and camera. I had been cautious about photographing the local people, especially as this area of Sumatra is strongly Muslim (intriguingly, the Minang Kabau people are also matriarchal, a strange combination) but I need not have bothered. A tiny grandmother holding her little granddaughter caught my eye and waved to me: 'Where from? Take photo? Sit, sit'. So I sat and snapped, duly admiring the baby until she waved me a friendly goodbye.

In the afternoon I went to a bullfight. In a soggy village field this Sumatran version of a bullfight was taking an eternity to start, which failed to bother the locals who were betting furiously with each other on the water buffalo that took their fancy. A Sumatran bullfight is a comparatively tame affair in which two buffalo lock horns until one of them gives up and turns tail. There were two contests, the first lasting five minutes, the second five seconds, as after a solid clash of heads one buffalo had had enough and ran out of the field and down the village

Going Ape in Sumatra

street, the other buffalo belting after it, men with ropes panting and shouting in its wake.

The guy who had run us out to the village in his transit van told us the significance of the bullfight to the people in this part of Sumatra, which gave the Minang Kabau tribe of the region their name.

'In the old times', he told us as we stood in the rain with several hundred wet Sumatrans, 'the Javanese came to invade our island but the people here in West Sumatra suggested a bullfight to decide who should be the winners. The Javanese agreed and brought their biggest bull. But the people here were clever. They took a young calf and starved it for a week before the contest. Then they tied a knife to its head, and when the calf saw the bull it was so desperate for food that it ran under the bull's stomach to try to find milk. The knife cut the bull and it died. Since then we have been called the Minang Kabau people, which means "Victory of the Bulls", and the bullfights have been held ever since.'

We continued our travels to Lake Toba and a different tribe – the Toba Bataks. I researched the tribe's background: 'The captive is bound to a stake in an upright position. A number of fires are lighted, the musical instruments are struck. Then the chief draws his knife, steps forward and addresses the people. It is explained that the victim is an utter scoundrel, not a human being at all but a *begu* (ghost) in human form, and the time has come for him to atone for his misdeeds. All draw their knives. The *raja* cuts off the first piece, being either a slice of the forearm or the cheek, if this be fat enough. He holds up the flesh and drinks with gusto some of the blood streaming from it. Then he hastens to the fire to roast the meat before devouring it. Now all the remaining men fall upon the bloody sacrifice, tear the flesh from the bones and roast and eat it. Some eat the meat raw, or half-raw to show off their bravery. The cries of the victim do not spoil their appetites. It is usually eight or ten minutes before the wounded man becomes unconscious, and a quarter of an hour before he dies.'

Justice, Toba Batak style, a traveller's account from 1840-1. They have not eaten anyone since . . . for several decades at least, I believe.

Intrepid Journeys

The most exotic thing I sampled while visiting Lake Toba, the sacred lake of the Batak people, was a goldfish. Not your average fishbowl tiddler, but a bulging carp that overlapped the plate like a six-foot man in a five-foot long bed. It came with a typical Indonesian sauce so hot that, for a few minutes, I actually lost the power of speech and my lips felt as if they had been plugged into the mains. I scraped off the coconut sauce and tucked into the tender flesh.

Breakfast next morning at the Rumba Pizzeria – by which time my lips had stopped tingling – was banana juice, a cup of coffee and a pancake so overstuffed with pieces of fresh papaya, pineapple and banana that it seemed to be smiling up at me from the plate. I was certainly smiling down at it as it was a sunny Sunday morning and I felt it was going to be a good day.

The Rumba Pizzeria is in the small and lazy resort of Tuk-Tuk, on Samosir Island in the middle of Lake Toba. Tuk-Tuk may be small but Samosir is not. It is about the size of Singapore, while Lake Toba is the largest crater lake in the world, bigger than the Dead Sea and thought to be one of the world's deepest lakes. It was created 75-100,000 years ago in what was probably the largest volcanic explosion the world has ever known, although the Bataks believe it was either made by their wrathful God, the Mulajadi Na Bolon (who created the world and then was cheated by the local people) or from the bitter tears of a sorrowful mother.

Sumatra has far fewer travellers than nearby Java, Bali and Borneo, so the prices are lower and the people much friendlier. As I walked along the coast road in Tuk-Tuk that sunny Sunday morning, one young man with a smile like the sunshine passed me saying, 'good morning, good Sunday, yes?' Earlier I had passed a store where a young lad with a guitar was entertaining some friends. It is hard to walk far in Sumatra without seeing someone with a guitar, or hearing a song. On the night I arrived I was tucking into my sweet-and-sour chicken, and my travelling companions were enjoying pizzas the size of hub caps, when from a grubby café across the street came the robust sound of Batak singing,

Going Ape in Sumatra

men's voices belting out in harmony, well-lubricated by palm wine. It sounded completely un-Asian, more like mournful but powerful fado or flamenco, crossed with a hint of 1950s doo-wop and South American rhythm.

'What are the songs about?' I asked the waitress.

'About love', was the inevitable reply. 'This one is how his girl went off with another man and now she is married to him and he is unhappy.'

'Any political songs?' I wondered.

'No, just love.'

Bob Marley is as much a modern musical hero in Sumatra as he is everywhere else in the world, and *Buffalo Soldier* was gently filling the air as I stopped for a Sprite on my Sunday morning stroll.

'Sit down, take a rest', invited Antonius, who was selling soft drinks in front of his *losmen*, or guesthouse. He owned six houses, he told me, all of them in traditional Batak style. These are high wooden houses with swooping triangular roofs, pointing forwards and upwards at the front and back. 'The back is usually a little higher than the front', Antonius explained, 'in the hope that children will be richer than their parents. The roofs used to be covered in *ijuk*, the fibres you get from the palm tree, but now it's usually zinc'. Less attractive but more practical, and the houses themselves are designed to be practical: they are raised from the ground to make room for water buffalo beneath, while the overhanging eaves provide shelter for rice-pounding and net-mending in the rainy season.

I took some photos, copied down Antonius's address so that I could send back some pictures for his photographic archive, and moved on, stopping to buy a piece of banana and chocolate cake from a little boy passing by, carrying a tin full of tempting slices that cost 500 rupiah (10 pence) for a hefty chunk. From the restaurant next door Bob Marley music still lazied out. Another boy walked by and said, 'good morning, yes?'

From across the harbour came the sound of a hymn, for the Bataks are Christian people. Sumatrans seem an incredibly adaptable race. The

Minangkabau people manage the unusual mix of being both Muslim and matriarchal, while the Toba Bataks became Christians under the Dutch while retaining their ancient beliefs, including animal sacrifice and ancestor worship.

'I still call in the medicine woman when my children are ill', Annette Silalahi told me. Annette is a German woman who came to Lake Toba several years ago and has never left. She married a local man, Anto, and together they run the Tabo vegetarian restaurant and bakery, as well as renting out cottages. 'The local healer is certainly at least as successful as conventional Western medicine', Annette insisted, while I wolfed down a sublime aubergine in a spicy coconut sauce, a thick slice of the bakery's bread and a big bottle of Bintang Beer.

Traditional remedies were evident too when we reluctantly moved on from Tuk-Tuk to Bukit Lawang, one of the most visited villages in Sumatra. The reason is orang hutan, the 'person of the forest', and the Bohorok Orangutan Rehabilitation Station, a short stroll away. 'The Station was opened in 1973 by two Swiss biologists', the Controller, Riswan Bangen, recounted, walking across his small office to take down a ledger from the shelves. He flipped through the pages, looking at figures. 'Since 1973, we have released 212 animals back into the wild. At the moment there are nine animals in quarantine, and fifteen using the feeding site.'

Just over 200 orphaned orangutans released back into the wild may not seem much but with only 5-7,000 orangutan on Sumatra and a declining world population of 30,000, every one of them matters. Those brought to Bohorok – the name of the river on which Bukit Lawang stands – have mostly been orphaned by hunters or kept as pets. They are kept in quarantine for six months, during which time they are taught never-acquired skills like climbing and nest-building. Once these vitally important necessities have been learnt, they are released into the semi-freedom of the Gunung Leuser National Park. Here they are fed twice daily, with visitors allowed to watch until their confidence returns – aided by the deliberately boring banana diet – and they head off, through

Going Ape in Sumatra

their own volition, to live in the jungle.

To visit the jungle requires a permit and the company of a local guide such as Nasib Suhardi, a handsome and amiable thirty-something Sumatran. 'It isn't easy to get a permit as a guide', he explained. 'You have to pass examinations, learn first aid and orienteering, and prove that you know the animals and plants.'

Orienteering is obviously a useful skill to possess when you are responsible for leading visitors through the dense jungle of a National Park which covers 2,500 square miles and contains tigers, snakes, rhinos, leopards, bears and the slightly less-dangerous (if you can find one) orangutan.

Nasib also knows his plants and traditional remedies; his father was a farmer and his mother a healer. 'My grandfather used to bring me into the jungle and tell me which plants were which, and what they did. This is the peacock fern, for instance', Nasib says, breaking off a leaf which looks to me just like any other fern. 'This can be used to heal bee stings.' Others cure nosebleeds or even nappy rash.

Nasib was a handy man to have in a jungle and proved equally adept at ape spotting too. I had been told there was really only a slim chance of seeing an orangutan in the wild and we were on our way back from the camp to Bukit Lawang on the second day of our brief trek with only a hint of an orangutan's call to our credit. Suddenly Nasib stopped us, peering up into the canopy of trees. Eventually a shape became evident, a shape which turned out to be a large and long-limbed male. To discourage humans, orangutans throw down branches, which this one duly did, and sometimes they . . . how to phrase this . . . choose to relieve themselves on the unlucky victim below. Luckily this one missed, as I think a T-shirt splattered in foul-smelling dung would have been an unfortunate souvenir. I cannot imagine the dry cleaner being too pleased to see me. Not far beyond the male with the magic bowels we then, to Nasib's delight as much as ours, came across two females, each with a baby clinging to her, but being ladies they merely threw a few branches down in our direction before swinging off through the treetops.

53

Intrepid Journeys

The aches in my legs disappeared and the sweat and leeches seemed a small price to pay for the privilege of seeing an endangered animal in the wild. We walked, exhausted but satisfied, back to Bukit Lawang, where I tucked straight into a huge plate of *pisang goreng* (fried bananas). Perhaps it was the influence of the orangutans but they certainly tasted delicious. Not quite as nice as a plump goldfish but much better than a scoundrel's cheek.

On The Road To Lhasa

by Steve Davey

A hundred pairs of eyes followed me around the cold, dark bus station. It was still only 5.00am and there was another hour to wait for the bus. I glanced over my shoulder to the rows of narrow, hard wooden benches, facing the now defunct departure board above my head. Everyone was staring at me with that implacable, unblinking gaze which I had grown accustomed to in China.

I walked on a few slow, casual paces and looked over my shoulder again. A hundred pairs of eyes had followed me. Five paces forwards and two paces to the left. The eyes had all followed me. Three paces backwards and turn. Yes, they were still looking. I was beginning to enjoy this. I was tempted to break into a song and dance routine or announce the immortal line 'I suppose you are wondering why I have called you here today?' but discretion, as always, gave in to valour. I did not speak enough Chinese to break into a speech, and one of the many squiggled signs lining every available space was bound to ban Frank Sinatra impersonations.

Intrepid Journeys

I could not really blame the crowd for staring. It was the coldest hour before dawn at Lanzhou bus station. There was nothing else to do and some of them had apparently been waiting since the previous night. Amongst the passengers were Chinese Muslims and a sprinkling of nomads from the town of Xiahe on the Tibetan Grasslands where I was heading. Very occasionally they would catch the bus to Lanzhou for shopping. Now, on top of all of the bizarre sights of the city they had a 6' 2" foreign devil wearing a giant People's Liberation Army greatcoat, indulging in a funny walk.

I was so looking forward to getting out of Lanzhou. Set in a long narrow valley, the town manages to trap all the noxious fumes and pollution from heavy industry further down the valley which hangs in a muddy yellow pall over the grey, ferroconcrete building. Dust and dirt blows down the streets, achieving terminal velocity before dashing itself into the faces of passing 'round-eyes' and gouging itself under contact lenses. Too many times in this town I had emerged from the eye-rubbing, pain-gyrating, mouth-open dance which is so familiar to contact lens wearers in dusty locations, to be faced by a large crowd of Chinese people staring at me with impenetrable interest.

To kill time I decided to take another prowl round the bus station. In one corner was a small shop offering to print stills from a video camera onto T-shirts. A souvenir from Lanzhou bus station. Needless to say the owner had no customers. This seemed to be a characteristic of the recently liberalised Chinese economy. Now anyone has the right to lose their shirt on dumb business ideas. A new freedom which many people are gratefully exploiting to the full.

It only seems to be the nature of the business not the nature of doing business which has changed in China. Even entrepreneurs have the same sullen reticence when it comes to serving the public that characterises services in state-run hotels and institutions like the railways. Ask for information or even try to buy something and you will often be treated like a puppy who has just left a stain on the carpet. After travelling in India, I would have thought that the lack of entreaties and impeachments from traders would be refreshing but it was actually

On The Road To Lhasa

rather unnerving. For probably the first time in Asia I felt unwanted!

Even the manner in which the departure announcement for my bus was made was uniquely Chinese. A female conductor, dressed in a tatty, faded blue uniform grabbed a signboard from a series of hooks on one side of the waiting room and swept across towards the appropriate bus with all the poise and arrogance which only a Chinese woman in a position of power can muster. The board above her head, she trailed passengers in her wake. Wakened from their cold and boredom- induced torpor they alternatively picked up luggage, dropped child, picked up child, dropped luggage as they scurried, legs bent after her, desperately trying to match her furious pace.

The bus station opened up onto a raised platform, level with the top of the bus, and the scramble to get luggage on board began. As well as the obligatory personal luggage, great bales of cloth, engine parts and even a couple of baskets of chickens were soon heaped on top of my rucksack.

There is always a problem on 'Third World' buses as to where to sit. Sit at the back and you will be thrown into the air with every bump. Sit at the front and you will be one of the first to die from the inevitable head-on collision *and* you will see it coming. Sit in the middle and you will be crushed by all the locals who have had Third World bus etiquette bred into them for generations. I opted to sit at the front where I would have a better view and more leg room, and settled into a seat which was so low that I had to stretch my legs over the engine cover to fit in.

For all the rush to get on the bus, it was another hour before the driver turned up – another hour to worry as to whether I was on the right bus, double-checking with passengers who did not speak English and fending off the stares of interested passers-by who were intrigued by the foreign devil sprawled half-on and half-off of his seat.

By now I was tired, cold and hungry – in just the right state of mind to eat my breakfast. The thin white plastic bag I clutched contained a couple of steamed dumplings. Now, when I travel I love to sample all the local food for lunch and dinner. Breakfast is a little different. Coffee and toast is about all I can manage. Steamed dumplings with a thin scrape of

Intrepid Journeys

sludgy green or muddy brown in the middle is more than I can face.

The driver whipped open his side door and swung himself into his seat. He looked over his shoulder at me and grinned. He looked Tibetan with his faintly red cheeks and short, spiky hair. He carried a large jam jar with coarse tea leaves in the bottom, which he regularly topped up with hot water throughout the journey. Every few minutes he would unscrew the lid, throw back his head and take a huge gulp.

The bus was half-full when the conductor climbed on to check the tickets. It was the same woman who had led the ragged procession through the bus station waiting room. Foreigners on buses from Lanzhou have to have two tickets – one for insurance following an international lawsuit from the family of a Japanese tourist who was killed in a bus crash, and one normal ticket which every traveller on a bus is required to hold. She seemed surprised that I had the right ticket and not a little disappointed. She still called various comments in Chinese over her shoulder for good measure, to the amusement of other passengers.

The engine howled and whined in protest as the driver crunched through the gears and the bus juddered off through the wakening streets of Lanzhou. I felt that surge of excitement that comes with the start of a new journey. Never mind the fact that in a few short hours it will turn to mind- and bottom-numbing boredom, it is the start of a journey which counts.

This excitement was heightened by seeing my first fight in China. Two rangy youths were throwing kid-in-the-playground style punches at each other with long, straight-armed shots with the head held back at an angle to keep it out of the way. One man had a bright red screwed-up face, whether the result of anger or receiving a number of punches I did not know. A small, jostling crowd had gathered and was attempting to restrain the combatants in a half-hearted, desultory fashion before the police arrived. I secretly knew how they felt. Lanzhou made me feel like punching someone; watching someone else do it was the next best thing.

As we pulled up out of the valley both the landscape and the mood changed. The bus seemed to stop at every opportunity for passengers to

On The Road To Lhasa

jump on and off. I had assumed my bus was providing a direct service but as more and more people crowded round me I realised it was going to be a longer journey than I had anticipated.

There appeared to be a large Muslim influence in this area of China. Minarets rose above small settlements along the route which owed more to pagodas than traditional Islamic architecture. If someone had told me that Antoni Gaudi was alive and well but had done a Cat Stevens and moved to China, I would not have been surprised.

We stopped on the outskirts of a large Muslim market town to allow three skinny individuals to haul a complete car engine onto the bus. Most of the passengers took the opportunity to climb off the bus and stock up on fruit for the rest of the trip, delaying the journey further.

The bus slowed to a crawl as we passed through the town. The roads were packed with Chinese Muslims. All seemed to be wearing identical grey tunics and embroidered hats. Traffic was slowed to a crawl which gave me a good view of the livestock area of the market which doubled as a *halal* slaughterhouse. Recalcitrant cattle were being pulled to the killing ground where they had their throats cut before being divided up.

Through the chaos a man in a clean white shirt appeared on a bicycle. Perfectly balanced, he was holding the handle bars with one hand while carrying a tray with what appeared to be a plateful of food and a glass of water with the other. He cut a surreal figure until the crowds swallowed up his weaving path.

On the other side of the street a funeral procession was forging its way against the flow of humanity. Five or six men carried an uncovered coffin on their shoulders. An old man lay in the coffin, his face the model of repose. A small group of mourners elbowed their way in pursuit.

The bus stopped on the other side of town for a lunch break of noodle soup and an opportunity to use the toilet which consisted of a hole in the floor of a rickety wooden outhouse which reeked of ammonia.

By the time we left the town the demographics of the bus changed. Most of the Muslim passengers had got off and the bus now seemed to be full of Tibetans. Tibetans are much larger in stature than the

Chinese, with more Caucasian features. A characteristic of the Tibetans is their red cheeks caused by diet and altitude, and as the bus climbed higher to the grasslands I could feel the tightening in my chest from the reduction of oxygen.

One newcomer to the bus was an old Tibetan man who carried an unhooded eagle on his arm. The bird did not seem to be concerned about the situation, rather it looked around with the same confident self-assurance I had once seen in the face of a pet fox that some tramp had carried on to the London Underground. 'I'm the only eagle on this bus – aren't you jealous of me?'

* * * * *

The 'flags of the dead' were fluttering viciously on the peaks of the brooding hills which ringed the town, as the cold wind swept from the Tibetan Plains down the valley, sweeping up the dust from the streets and dashing it in the face of the monks and the nomadic pilgrims who were struggling up to the sprawling Prabang Monastery.

All around the three kilometre perimeter of the monastery were prayer wheels, forming a route for the faithful. Groups of nomads from the grasslands, which stretch from just outside Xiahe to Lhasa in Tibet, were trudging round – always clockwise – spinning each of the great, heavy wheels in turn whilst reciting prayers. Periodically on the pilgrimage route was a small building containing an extra large prayer wheel. Old women struggled to turn this great wheel before hurrying after their families.

The more devout were prostrating themselves in front of the large prayer wheels, throwing themselves down repeatedly onto sheepskin rugs. This included a couple of old women whose faith was more important to them than their arthritis as they struggled up and down, using the steps as support.

Two men were cheerfully making a circuit of the perimeter, prostrating themselves, reaching out to full stretch, standing up and then prostrating themselves all over again. Each time they advanced no more than a metre, meaning that they had to repeat the process over three

On The Road To Lhasa

thousand times to complete one circuit. They had well-worn pads fixed to their knees and elbows. Whatever the reason for their penance, they were joking and laughing.

I learnt later that people often come to make a circuit like this in order to request a successful conception, or to offer their thanks for a granted wish or to atone for some misdeed. There is even rumour of a pilgrimage where penitents prostrate themselves all the way across the grasslands to Lhasa which is reputed to take nine years, although no one I spoke to had ever met anyone who had ever completed it.

Dressed in huge yak skin jackets, the nomads are a fearsome sight – especially as I had been told by a local that there is no word in their language for 'sorry'. The sleeves of their coats reach down to the ground in order to protect their hands from the bitter cold. Traditionally – for working or fighting – the coats are generally worn off one shoulder with the fur-lined collar and hood hanging halfway down their backs. Some of these are lined with the skins of the rare Clouded Leopard, an endangered species, still valued by the nomads for their skins.

For all their wild-eyed looks and the fierce knives they wear at their belts, the nomads are remarkably friendly. I had expected some lawless frontier town but was surprised to see families of nomads in earnest and animated discussion, sitting at tables in cafés and restaurants throughout town. They presented an incongruous sight in their traditional costumes, designed for survival in tents on the inhospitable plains not Xiahe café society.

Xiahe is an important Tibetan pilgrimage site. The monastery was decimated in the cultural revolution and has only recently been reformed, whether for reasons of genuine liberalisation or propaganda.

The next day I was up before the sun to head out into the grasslands with Man Su, a local who was born in the grasslands and whose grandfather still lives out there. We were driving out to the Mo'Ar Monastery which has recently been renovated and has received few foreign visitors.

I was taking Man Su as a guide because the grasslands can be a dangerous place. The danger is not just from the nomads, although they are quick to respond to even an unintentional slight, but from their dogs. These are huge, great, hairy, fearsome beasts which the nomads keep to protect their encampments and women when the menfolk are away grazing their yak herds for months on end during the summer. The dogs run wild and often form packs. Vicious on their own, they are lethal in packs. They seem to leave the nomads alone but only two weeks earlier a pack had set upon and killed a French tourist who was walking alone. She was so badly mauled she was barely recognisable. The Chinese army had been brought in and shot many of the stray dogs – the nomads were still smarting from the insult.

On the way out to the grasslands Man Su told me more about the lives of the nomads. The grasslands, which to us look so open, are in reality divided into pockets owned by different clans. If a yak from one clan strays into the territory of another, it will be stolen. The clan which loses the yak will launch a raid to try to recover it and a battle will ensue. Some dozen nomads a year are killed in this way and many others injured. The authorities tend to turn a blind eye. The grasslands are not exactly lawless but it is nomad law which runs them and that is a law which allows for vendettas and blood feuds.

Man Su also told me that the nomads are not polygamous but neither are they monogamous. During the enforced separation every summer, both men and women are able to take lovers. This is not regarded as a bad thing, it just happens. The women apparently know enough natural remedies to prevent conception during their time with their lover, but if a woman should conceive, her husband will raise the child as his own.

Our first stop was a nomad tent pitched in the grasslands. I had to wait in the car as Man Su nervously got out to speak to the nomads to see if they would invite us into their home. More importantly, I wanted to wait until they had kicked their dogs into submission. I was scared enough of them before I met Man Su. After he showed me scars from when he was savaged by a dog which shredded his arm only the year before, I was doubly convinced. I need not have worried. Man Su had brought gifts of bread from the town and that, combined with their innate sense of hospitality, soon won over the nomads.

On The Road To Lhasa

Inside the tent, which was woven from Yak hair, we were served Yak milk tea by a nomad woman. Cooked over a fire-stove, the tea tasted smoky but drove the cold from my bones. I swapped questions with the nomad family, who seemed as interested in me as I was in them, making it difficult to tear ourselves away.

The Mo'Ar Monastery is a long and hard sixty kilometre drive across the striking scenery of the plains, already lightly dusted with snow in the shadows. On the way we called at some of the nomads' winter quarters. The dwellings have courtyards enclosed by high walls to keep the families' livestock safe and sheltered. In the spring the families close up their winter dwelling and once more take to the plains to graze the Yaks, goats and sheep.

Walking through the small town next to the monastery was like going back in time. So far away from anything which passed as civilisation there was no electricity or telephones. Everyone was dressed in enormous nomad clothes and mine was the only motor vehicle. Horse-drawn carts were coming in from the plains loaded high with fodder to feed the livestock throughout the harsh winter months. They made stately, imponderous progress as they drifted timelessly in from the plains – sometimes with one or two people perched precariously on top of the swaying load.

Man Su was getting more and more nervous as I walked about taking photographs, but the nomads were accepting my presence good-humouredly. Winter was looming and this was a pleasant diversion for them. Many of the nomads out here had never seen Westerners before, although they had heard rumours of strange foreign devils. Now here was one, running around with a camera, wearing antique Chairman Mao sunglasses and an army greatcoat. They were more amused than offended.

I was certainly causing quite a stir. I had come to stare at the nomads but they were certainly going to stare at me. The more time I spent on the grasslands, the more I was finding the normal rules of tourism overturned. I had come to look and to question but I was finding myself looked at and comprehensively questioned.

One of the monks saw my approach and invited us into the monastery. His name was Danzin and he was thirty-six years old. He had a permanent, broad smile which seemed to fill his entire face, making his eyes crinkle shut. He took us around some of the renovated buildings, carefully avoiding making any comments as to why they needed renovation. It was, of course, because of the excesses of the Cultural Revolution when anything 'old' and anything 'religious' was destroyed by chanting, pre-pubescent Red Guards – which is why even such an out of the way monastery was so comprehensively vandalised. The Cultural Revolution, just like the situation in Tibet and the exile of the Dalai Lama, was a guilty secret; a pretence that no one needs to mention, because everybody knows what is being alluded to.

We were invited back to Danzin's cell where he detailed some junior monks to boil up some yak milk, then he made us more of the ubiquitous tea and *sambar*, a paste made from black bean flour, yak butter, sugar and water – the staple diet of the locals. As we ate, he bombarded me with questions about my home and my life. When I could, I slipped in a few questions in of my own. Life was hard but he managed to have a few luxuries. His small cell was in one of the newer parts of the monastery and would have resembled a wooden holiday cabin were it not for the fact that he had to stay in it for the entire bitter winter. He had a selection of photographs up on his wall, including his family and a selection of Lamas and, of course, the Dalai Lama. An old and battered ghetto blaster was his prized possession, which he claimed was there to help him learn his chants. I pressed him as to whether he had any more modern music and he blushed coyly, maintaining it was used for divine purposes alone. Scrabbling around in a drawer he produced a cassette which turned out to be Tibetan chants, a suitable background to our conversation. Word had spread of my presence and a number of younger apprentices kept poking their heads around the door of the cell, laughing as if daring each other to enter or say something. Every so often one would come flying in – pushed by his peers – grin nervously and then exit quickly to sounds of hushed recriminations outside.

On The Road To Lhasa

Danzin asked if we had Buddhist monks in the West. I hedged a yes but chose not to point out that they were generally either pretentious yuppies or superstars alleged to abuse rodents. He explained that the Mo'Ar Monastery used to be much larger but now only held some six hundred monks. It is 2,200 kilometres from Lhasa in Tibet, four days by car. Most of the monks were working at renovations to the monastery, helped by devout nomads.

Apparently there was only one part of the monastery which was not destroyed in the Cultural Revolution. This was a large academy and although the building had been taken over and used for housing livestock, most of the precious scrolls and religious artifacts had been preserved. Danzin said that no visitors, Western or Chinese, had been allowed in since the Cultural Revolution. He was prepared to show us around but I was not to take any pictures.

The interior of the academy belied its modest exterior. Ornate wall coverings and paintings covered all available space, and cushions for the monks to sit on whilst learning the tenants of their faith were strewn across the floors. Great racks of scrolls filled one wall. Originally there were four academies at the monastery for the four disciplines which the monks need to learn, including medicine and calligraphy. Now only this academy exists.

Yak butter candles provided the only light, filling the air with their potent smell and reminding me of the local delicacy which I had eaten the night before, a whole chicken cut up and fried in special spices and cooked in yak butter and greens. It tasted delicious but with the head and beak hanging over one end of the plate and the feet hanging over the other it was a bit too complete for my taste.

Danzin took us through a small door on the far wall into the inner sanctum of the temple. I caught Man Su's eye and he looked visibly moved. More than me, he realised the significance of being allowed to see this. A huge golden Buddha dominated the room, dwarfing everything else. It was said to be used for telling the futures of believers. The smell of Yak butter in this room was overpowering.

One wall was covered with small niches, each filled with a tiny

Buddha statue. These had been brought by pilgrims from all over the grasslands. On another wall was a collection of priceless scrolls. These had remained hidden for years and were far too precious for novice monks to read.

Danzin explained that the monastery had been founded nine generations ago and that the remains of each of the previous nine abbots were kept here for veneration. Again, they had been hidden during the Cultural Revolution by the faithful, who risked great persecution for upholding their beliefs. This was, without doubt, the most holy part of the monastery and whether it was this thought or the soporific effect of the Yak butter candles, I felt a palpable sense of peace washing over me.

Every journey should have a beginning and an end and I felt that this was a fitting end – not just for my journey from Xiahe but for my time in China. You never know when the end of a journey will come but you should keep going until you find that complete moment of realisation. When travelling it is easy to simply see something for its tourist value alone, overlooking the contribution it makes to those whose lives are affected by it: to look at the Great Wall and imagine it being visible from space rather than considering the individuals who built and defended it; to see buildings such as the Mo'Ar or Prabang Monasteries and to forget the lives which have been intertwined with them. Lives of devotion and lives of persecution.

Just surviving on the grasslands is difficult enough for the nomads, yet they still have time for their faith – to make pilgrimages and even to help renovate the monastery; to greet and welcome strange and bizarre visitors such as myself. We take our lives and our possessions so seriously, it is humbling to spend even a small amount of time with people who have a different set of values. I thanked Danzin with a completely inadequate *shadak* and headed back into the weak and waning sunlight which heralded the onset of winter. I felt a great sense of relief. I had had my moment of realisation. It was time to go home.

Sucking Eggs In Burma

by Peter Robinson

Make a small hole at one end of egg. Purse lips. Raise egg to lips, suck. Enjoy.

I was being given a quick lesson in how to suck eggs. It was 2.00am – give or take a few hours – and here at a tiny railway station the locals were snacking on raw eggs with their green tea.

Our train's defective locomotive lay idle, long since abandoned by the driver and it sat motionless in the darkness.

The road to Mandalay would be a long one.

★ ★ ★ ★ ★

After a few idle days in Burma's capital, Rangoon – or, if one prefers, the ruling SLORC's new names, Myanmar and Rangoon respectively – I was booked in to test the country's transport infrastructure. Surely the disaster stories I had heard were exaggerations? I was eternally optimistic about a punctual arrival in Mandalay (name unchanged) the following morning (Burma time – subject to alteration).

It is always a good sign, or at least a sign, that Myanmar Railways has

Intrepid Journeys

always had the best intentions, when the train leaves on time. That is what Bernard said, any way. Bernard (the Burmese call him Chuck Norris) had led small group trips through the country on many occasions and knew the system. Maybe it was his added disclaimer I thought puzzling. 'There's plenty of time for things to go wrong', he said, raking his fingers through his straggly mop of blond hair. 'You'll see what I mean', he added darkly. I was already confused by the name-changing.

The bustle of Rangoon railway station seemed impossibly chaotic. It was a bit like a crowd scene from *Ghandi*, except we had got tickets and did not have to clamber aboard the locomotive. We threaded our way through the mass of humanity to the platform's iron gates. A uniformed official was checking everyone's papers thoroughly but as soon as he looked up and saw us, he immediately waved us past the agitation. I guess they expect foreigners rather than locals to travel.

The promise of a sleeper carriage had changed name and identity to become a comfy seat, similar to those vinyl recliners from the early 1960s. But hell, it was only a twelve-hour journey. Bernard - Chuck Norris – quietly joked that the army generals had probably pinched our sleeper carriage for themselves.

Apart from our little group, there were a few Burmese businessmen and a couple of young soldiers casually stowing their machine guns. They recognised Chuck and made fun of his long, unruly hair and straggly beard. After all, was that not him staring down from the billboards outside every Rangoon movie theatre?

I strolled through the dining car where boxes of food were being hurriedly stored, while on the floor a fire burned untended in a cut-down 44-gallon drum, the top of which held a steel grid and blackened cooking wok. Nice fire hazard, I thought to myself.

The next carriage had wooden straight-backed benches crammed with three passengers (or four if they were really friendly) abreast of the aisle. There was not a vacant space anywhere. Bags, parcels and boxes of all sizes were stowed overhead, under feet and on knees. I tried looking nonchalant at the scene and decided to check the rest of the train later.

At 6.31pm we clanked and screeched our steel wheels out of Rangoon and headed for high adventure on the road to Mandalay.

Sucking Eggs in Burma

Night fell quickly, the sights of trackside shanty towns, rural villages and fields replaced by glimpses of life in Burma's ramshackle wooden homes and backstreets. Dim yellow globes cast pools of light in the enveloping blackness. Rangoon Station snack food was munched, the alternative – fried rice, curry or noodles – served beautifully in Big Mac style polystyrene containers, or the ubiquitous plastic bag, by our carriage steward. Relative values of peanuts, biscuits and chocolate were discussed. Biscuits got the thumbs down except for Bernard's, which were of the choc-coated variety. Where on earth did he get them?

Breakfast orders were taken. I decided to skip my companions' preference for French Toast and opted, without knowing its contents, for the standard breakfast box.

The idle clatter of the train's wheels turned to regular violent jolting courtesy of irregular tracks. I contemplated the region's history, in particular the fate of the PoWs in World War II, who were enslaved to build Burma's railway and wondered if this track was part of the wartime labour. If it was, then the railway was still making the Aussies suffer.

Our train slowed and pulled into a siding to let another one rocket past on the main line. No wonder it takes twelve hours to travel four hundred odd kilometres – this must be the slowest express to anywhere. The actual distance remains a mystery; I bought a map in Rangoon but no mileage rules were incorporated.

The locomotive hesitantly ground its burden onwards and I looked out of the window to judge the speed . . . it seemed like walking pace.

More hours of low speed bouncing and swaying. I could not read or write legibly. Finally, with a resounding convulsion, the train halted and backed into a siding. An announcement was made in Burmese, followed by a collective moan from our fellow Burmese travellers. Bernard disappeared into the next carriage and returned. He thought someone had said that the locomotive needed repairs. How long? No one knew.

We dozed. Fans circulated humid air, complete with a mini-bombardment of insects attracted by the dim fluorescent lights. Six hours into a great train journey and I was sitting zombie-like as around me snores indicated human resignation. My bladder was bursting so I dismounted the carriage tentatively, walked towards the loco and dared

Intrepid Journeys

to show my disdain by relieving myself on a big steel wheel.

After the stuffiness of the train, stretching my legs felt good. A nearby voice startled me. From the darkness a figure approached and spoke with a thick accent.

'You speak English? Good. This loco is finish, must wait for new one to come. It will come maybe two hours, maybe six. When it come'. He shrugged resignedly. He knew the system. I was having trouble adjusting to it.

My new friend was a young Pakistani businessman from Rangoon, heading for Mandalay to sell middle-of-the-road watches. He pointed down the tracks to where a tiny country station radiated the only sign of life in this broken-down journey. 'Come, we will have drink, yes?' But the train, what would happen if the train was suddenly fixed and left without me? However, one look at the inanimate Chinese-built loco reassured me that it had really expired.

By now it was 12.30am. I was in the middle of nowhere at a Burmese country railway station. What was I doing here? I was not alone though – the platform was still crowded with disconsolate people showing all the body language of passengers who had a long wait ahead of them. A blue fog rose from the coarse tobacco the men smoked, children slept in their mothers' arms, chickens huddled in wicker cages and a few voices disturbed the thick night.

In the distance a train whistle pieced the calm and my heart skipped a beat. Was this our replacement loco? Eventually a single light appeared and minutes later, with a roar, an express train swept past. Lucky bums . . . they got a train that worked.

My friend guided me towards a little tea room. He knew the ropes, this smooth-talking business-suited salesman. We found a little table to sit at – 'little' being the operative word in Burma. My first encounter with miniature stools in Rangoon had me thinking that they were catering for hordes of children. It was like practicing the squat position on a nine-inch high wooden stool.

Perhaps I would like to sell my watch, my friend enquired. He offered me a vast sum, 1,000 kyats, for my new Swatch. It had cost me $45.00. Now, my friend, you are not quite as cool a dude as you think you are. He then asked me to come to the opening of his new shop in

Sucking Eggs in Burma

Rangoon, all the right people would be there and his wife's uncle was a general in the army.

We drank. I had learned to choose tea in Burma as the coffee inevitably comes strong and sickly-sweet with an inch of sweetened condensed milk sludge at the bottom of a pyrex glass. Mister Cool's darting eyes caught me staring at the next table. I could not believe my eyes – the locals were snacking on raw eggs! An egg is broken onto a saucer, the rim is then held to the lips and the contents noisily slurped down. One of the guys at the next table carefully cracked the top of one egg, picked away a circle of shell, pierced the membrane, brought the hole to his lips and sucked, leaving albumen stringing down his chin. A spoon deftly loosened the recalcitrant bits from the shell and it soon descended to chase the yolk.

'You like to have egg?' Mister Cook inquired and immediately made the double kissing noise to summon the waiter. Before I could refuse, he seemed to have ordered two eggs. How could I get out of this one without offending the dark-suited salesman sitting opposite me? I did not want to end up with egg on my face but two eggs arrived, rolling around on their saucers. Mister Cool proceeded to chip away at the top of his egg. With a loud suck and a gulp, the contents were swallowed. A quick wipe of the mouth, a lick of the lips, the job was done. He looked at my egg and then at me. 'Go right ahead – you have it', I was thinking, but I gingerly picked away at the shell, explaining that this not the custom in Australia, that we prefer our eggs cooked. 'You must try', he insisted, 'is very good'. Now this was a dare. I lifted the hole to my lips and . . . I could not do it. The thought of experimenting with raw eggs at 2.00am had me gagging.

My friend smiled. Never one to waste food, he took my egg and vacuumed it clean. We laughed, accompanied by chortles from all corners of the tea room. Every one had eyes on this stranger. Another train thundered past. The tea room nightclub returned to normal and joint was still humming at 4.00am. I paid my 50 kyats and stepped outside.

Time for a reality check. I was in Burma, stuck in the middle of nowhere with my buddies and transport lying silent a little way up the tracks. If they were still there. Glancing up the lines I could not really

Intrepid Journeys

make out a train in the darkness. Panic. I walked quickly along the tracks, found the train, counted the carriages to find home. Wait, there was no locomotive. Damn, was this my train?

I climbed aboard and discovered unfamiliar faces in the dim emergency-lit carriages. Next carriage, Western faces. Chuck Norris stirred. I returned to my seat and stared up a the light globe covered in insects. The fetid air of confined humanity assaulted my nasal membranes and ever so gently, mosquitoes landed on my exposed flesh. After hours of semi-comatose rest, I checked my watch and found only twenty-five minutes had passed; then sleep came.

What was that? A jolt? There were voices outside, a deep throbbing engine, metallic clanking and then another jolt. Our replacement had arrived. Daylight appeared and ghostly figures were making themselves busy up and down the tracks. Full carriage lighting came on, passengers stirred and an announcement was made – not that it was any use to us as it was in Burmese.

Ten minutes later the loco revved up, followed by a succession of clunks from the carriage couplings and then the train ground down the long road to Mandalay. Breakfast smells emitted from the dining car. An hour later French Toast was distributed to my companions who had found it the preferable choice the night before. My breakfast pack arrived – cold, oily fried egg, bread and cram cheese. An hour's sleep had not prepared me for this and my stomach turned.

The hours passed as slowly as the train's velocity. We pulled into another siding and stopped. Another announcement in Burmese. People poured off the train and stood on the adjacent tracks. A perfectly normal thing to do at 8.00am in the middle of the Burmese countryside.

Thirty minutes later a uniformed railway official waved everyone back on board and we began moving again. By 10.00am I was feeling a bit peckish after seeing barbecued chicken pass within inches of my nose. As I bumped my way past the seats to the next carriage, one of my companions told me I was too late, there was no food left.

'What? No food?'
'Nope, nothing, zilch, zero.'
'Ah well, a bottle of water then.'
'Umm, no water either.'

Sucking Eggs in Burma

At 11.00am we ground to a halt at a station, everyone making a dash for the platform tea rooms, with me right at the front of the crush. I found some sweet pastry-type-things for which I have never discovered a name or ingredients. The first couple hit the spot and were washed down with tepid tea. I watched as passengers bargained with kids selling plastic bags of dubious-looking yellow curry, and younger children pleaded with passengers for empty water bottles.

Without warning the train started pulling out of the station. The panic was on. I grabbed a handful of kyats, slapped them down on the counter and sprinted for the nearest open carriage door and with a leap of faith jumped across the ever-widening gap between platform and train. Nice game, mister engine driver! Bet he gets a kick out of that every time.

However, the adrenaline rush did not last long. Lethargy returned promptly along with the same old violent motion, and my addled brain could not rid itself of the thought that no countryman of mine would lay trackwork this bad.

In the meantime, my companions who had breakfasted on French Toast were turning green. One by one they headed for the small compartment with the tiny hole in the floor, coming back clutching wrung-out stomachs and looking decidedly the worse for wear. I was feeling better, quite cheerful in fact; it is not often that fate deals me a good hand on a railway journey. I cast a furtive glance at my breakfast pack, glad that its contents had remained intact.

'We should be there by 12.00 at this rate', Chuck informed me. 'But whether it's 12.00 midday or 12.00 midnight I'm not saying. Heh, heh.' Despite an allotment of good fortune, my sense of humour seemed to have suffered at the hands of Myanmar Railways.

Now six hours overdue in Mandalay, the Burma bullet-train speared across the dry countryside at walking pace. There was a distinct possibility that the following day's train may beat us to our destination.

Mid afternoon. It was sweltering, the last of our water was gone. If anyone finds this note, could they please inform my next-of-kin. I took some photos as evidence of our mistreatment in Burma.

4.00pm. Some signs of civilisation. Buildings and road transport passed thick and fast and Bernard announced that we had arrived. At

Intrepid Journeys

5.00pm the train shuddered to a final halt. No one gave a second thought to leaving our home of the last twenty-two-and-a-half hours. Scrambling off, I caught a glimpse of Mister Cool who just nodded slowly and smiled.

Was this a new record for the Mandalay Express – twenty-two-and-a-half hours instead of twelve? Chuck Norris stroked his beard and pondered. 'It could be', he answered, 'but it runs a close race with a previous trip when three carriages accidentally detached themselves from the main train and were left behind for several hours. Fourteen hours from Thahze to Rangoon, a far shorter distance than from Rangoon to Mandalay'.

We found a local tray-back taxi and climbed aboard, heading to another tea room for refreshments and clean toilets. We drank our tea, ate, stretched our limbs and boarded a small bus for our next destination, Maymyo, in the mountains close to the Burma-China border. The road was rutted, narrow, potholed. Hard seats and numb buttocks. We travelled for five hours up steep switch-back roads in total darkness. My fellow passengers should have turned into zombies by now, if they felt anything like I did.

We arrived in Maymyo and drove around, unable to find the guest house. We asked locals, got lost, found the guest house, grabbed our luggage and were horizontal in minutes. Sleep came swiftly but with a steady rocking motion.

* * * * *

Warm sunshine lifted the morning fog from my travel-weary bones, simultaneously revealing Maymyo's quiet streets, its beautiful Burmese teak villas and majestic, decaying British mansions from the colonial days.

Already, the cool crisp air faintly echoed with everyday sounds as the hilltop town's market came to life. Traders staked out their patches of dirt, spreading their produce in neat rows on squares of faded hessian. Burma's fast food outlets – a cooking pot on a smoky fire – doled out watery yellow curry in plastic bags in exchange for a few kyat notes. Coffee and tea was also served in plastic bags but included a straw. I wondered how curry could be consumed from a plastic bag without any implements.

Today's special: freshly picked strawberries for 15 kyats a punnet. It was too early for dessert so Chuck Norris took us to an Indian tea room where the tandoori oven churned out delicious steaming hot naan and wonderfully sweet strawberry jam (and dahl for those in need of a curry fix). Naan with melted cheese and sugar was offered by the snaggle-toothed dough-boy . . . hot, sweet and a little greasy, it slid over the tongue comfortingly, as only fatty and sugary things can. We loved it.

The local transport here was either World War II vintage clapped-out Willys jeeps (half of which had their bonnets up while drivers poured endless quantities of fluids into semi-expired smoking and steaming motors) or a taxi rank of ancient stage coaches drawn by clapped-out, bony ponies. Count the ribs, count the bald tyres.

A few days later we were heading through the dry, dusty plains towards Pagan, site of Burma's ancient capital, on kidney-bruising roads in a bus with no suspension. However, all was forgiven – even the night's mosquito plague – as I stood high up on the edge of a pagoda and the first ray of dawn light broke the horizon. A blaze of fiery orange transformed the panorama and a thousand pagodas loomed from the misty Irrawaddy river valley.

Burma's transport system then took another step backwards. We hired a boat with a smoking, chugging engine which gave its death rattle mid-stream of the Irrawaddy. The pleasure cruise reverted to a pleasure drift until our stricken craft was towed ashore and we were forced to walk a long way home along the riverbanks.

Returning to Mandalay, I sat in the Nylon Ice Cream parlour, devouring scoops of creamy strawberry ice cream. The place was a magnet to Mandalysians and tourists alike, and I chatted to fellow travellers from all parts of the globe. Tales of transport woes came thick and fast but so did stories of the refreshing friendliness of the Burmese.

Our return to Rangoon was imminent. My mood changed to that of a tooth-ache patient awaiting a dental appointment. I pondered on the safety record of Mandalay Air's ageing Fokkers. However, the hour was nigh and our funeral procession solemnly boarded the overnight express to Rangoon, sharing a carriage already crowded with smiling camouflage-clad soldiers toting AK-47s. To lighten the mood, Chuck Norris played bookmaker on the chance of our arrival on time. 'Within two hours of schedule is almost unheard of. Nearest, to the hour, not day – heh, heh – wins a prize', he decided.

The loco set a cracking pace on a good head of diesel fumes and sleep came fitfully. Daylight. French Toast was not the breakfast order on this part of the journey. Like boy scouts we had come prepared and packets of food were broken open and shared: salty potato crisps, pastries, Chuck's choc-coated wafer biscuits and water.

I had a great view of the dining car's rear end wobbling along the tracks. The drum cooking fire was smoking and I imagined plastic bags of French Toast being distributed along the adjoining carriages. Boy, they were cooking a lot of stuff. Smoke billowed from the doorway, streaming into our carriage. Flames flickered in the blackness, there was some yelling and people rushed out of the dining car. The train was now, officially, on fire. Smells of wood and bitumen floor burning wafted through and then finally the smoke turned grey and clouds of stream emerged. The blaze had been extinguished.

Our journey never faltered and we hurtled through the Burma plains at breakneck speed on twisted rails as carriages shuddered their protest.

I stared at the charred rear of the dining car, thinking this was a fitting end to my tales of woe on the Burma railway. There was a perceptible change in our impetus now – ramshackle houses and Burma's frenetic, unruly road traffic appeared to be heavier.

Our 8.00am arrival time had just ticked over. Within twelve minutes the Rangoon Express rattled into its station terminus. My thrill rides on Burma's time warp transport were complete. I had lost my bet with Chuck. The winner won a one-way ticket to Nirvana on the Mandalay Express. Heh, heh.

Temples In The Jungle

by Juliet Coombe

Emerging from the tragedy of recent political turmoil and bloodshed, the road from Phnom Penh (the capital of Cambodia) to Siem Reap is living proof of the destruction of Pol Pot's revolutionary reign from 1975-9. Most villages and farms lie in ruin. At every twist and turn in the road one sees buildings so dismembered that their past function is totally unrecognisable. As one *Guardian* journalist put it recently: 'Going to Siem Reap, it could be said that one was travelling through ruins in order to reach ruins'.

To fully understand the brutality of Pol Pot's rule, I hired a bicycle in order to visit the infamous Tuol Sleng and the Killing Fields. When I reached the former I shivered as I stared through the barbed wire, reading a sign on Building C warning prisoners that the wire barricade had been erected there to prevent them from committing suicide. Closing my eyes I believed I could hear the screams of the prisoners and felt totally desolate in one of the world's largest ever detention and torture centres. It was hard to imagine that Tuol Sleng had once been

Tuol Svay Prey, Cambodia's leading high school pre-1975.

Pol Pot's security forces soon put a stop to this, converting the school into a chamber of horrors. The place became known as Security Prison 21 (S-21) and I wondered, as I walked through the doors, how such a place of evil could have existed for so long.

During the height of Pol Pot's power anyone who was brought to this jail knew their death warrant had been signed. An average of one hundred people were tortured daily during the latter half of the 1970s. When the spirit had been smashed and the prisoner was too weak to even talk, he was taken to the extermination camp at Choeung Ek to be executed. Life was cheaper than the paper on which their names appeared and no one really knows the exact number of prisoners who passed through these gates.

Even now the place felt like a graveyard. Nothing stirred and the only noise came from my shoes as they echoed across the cold stone floors. It was hard to tell whether the single cells on the ground floor were worse than the second floor's mass detention area. Somehow, I thought that in a prisoner's last hours any form of company would have been better than none at all, particularly as the single rooms had nothing more than a wrought iron bed, to which victims' arms and legs were tied; the grey walls added to the morbidity, creating the impression of being in a compression chamber. Black and white photographs show only too vividly the crimes of the Khmer Rouge. In some rooms the walls are still stained with blood and the lack of air, combined with the dank smell, made me wonder why so many tourists are attracted to spending their holidays in such places; a prison where an estimated 17,000 men, women, children as young as two, and nine Westerners were bludgeoned to death between 1975 and 1978.

As I made my way back to my bike, propped up against the outer wall of the prison, I noticed a dead sparrow and thought nothing could survive here. Back on my bike I watched a coachload of tourists arrive, alighting from the bus, cameras swinging from their necks. They seemed excited about seeing this genocidal monument, discussing Pol Pot as if he was some kind of modern day Hollywood hero rather than an evil

Temples in the Jungle

tin-pot dictator, responsible for the deaths of over a million of Cambodia's seven million people. The words of my hotelier echoed in my head: 'Every one of us has lost a member of our family and we do not see the last two decades of continual warfare as a tourist attraction. It is a period we want obliterated from our daily lives, instead of being constantly reminded of it by gung-ho happy-snappy tourists wearing T-shirts saying "Legless in Cambodia". What happened is not a joke and we will never forget it.'

Fifteen kilometres on, standing in the middle of the Killing Fields, it was incredible to think that this picturesque farming land hid a terrible secret. Under a sea of paddy fields are the remains of 8,985 people who were found bound, blindfolded and buried in 129 communal graves. I understood why the people of Cambodia wanted this period of history buried forever. So horrific was it that the only way forward is to place it firmly in the past.

The Killing Fields orchard, as it is now known, is centred around a memorial stupa erected in 1988. Through the clear glass windows of the stupa, one can bear witness to over 8,000 dismembered heads. A local boy explained that the skulls are ordered by size and positioned on trays so that they can look out across the fields scattered with fragments of their bones. All around the site the local farmers plough the fields with rice in an attempt to put these revolutionary years behind them, but they, nevertheless, continue to live in fear of land mines that scatter the length and breadth of the country and, worse still, the possible return of the Khmer Rouge.

I returned to the centre of town and went to the Foreign Correspondents Club (FCCS) for a quiet drink. Sipping a gin and tonic, looking out at Phnom Penh's tranquil waterfront, I found it hard to believe that Cambodia is still very much at war with the Khmer Rouge. My silent reflection did not last long, shattered by a boy being narrowly missed by a car as he hobbled across the road to take up his well established begging position outside the club. This boy had not lost his leg through being reckless, he was one of hundreds of thousands of Cambodian land mine victims.

Intrepid Journeys

Cambodia, according to the British Mines Advisory Group, is peppered with an estimated ten million land mines. At least three hundred people a month are blown apart by old mines. While some are killed instantly, others have to live a life with lost limbs. The boy looked up at me, sitting on the balcony, and grinned cheekily. I was amazed. He could not join the other boys across the road playing football – the only occupation left for this nine year old was begging and scavenging. During further visits to the FCCS, I always saw him holding his own, smiling, whilst begging in several different languages with those who came and went from the club.

A day did not pass when he did not have a word of advice or a flattering comment for me. He was very knowledgeable about his country and advised me to take the boat to Siem Reap, a particularly beautiful journey at this time of year. 'The rainy season makes everything lush and green, turning Cambodia from a brown, burnt-out dust bowl into a tropical Eden', he said, smiling as he handed me a orchid. Each day he gave me a different flower, and so our friendship blossomed as I exchanged books for fascinating anecdotes about this beautiful yet tragic country.

The day before I planned to take the boat journey, he offered to buy my ticket for US$20.00. Everyone said I was crazy to trust a street child but early the next morning I heard a rattle at my window. 'The boat, the boat', shouted the boy. 'It is leaving at 6.00, not 7.00am. You must hurry or you will miss it.' I grabbed my bags and hailed a passing truck. The boy dragged himself into the back, behind me, and off we went, hurtling down the back streets at frightening speed.

As we passed the Grand Palace and the main section of the waterfront, the boy handed me my boat ticket and, to my surprise, US$5.00 in change. He smiled and explained, 'the locals only pay US$15.00'. Feeling terribly ashamed for ever doubting the child's honesty, I tried to hand back the money. This gesture greatly offended him. Looking at my held out hand, he turned his back on me saying, 'we are friends, are we not?' The truck driver wrenched the gears yet again, sending us both flying as the vehicle moaned and snarled to a halt. Out

Temples in the Jungle

I leapt, pushing the truck to try and jump-start it down the broken road, as dust flew in every direction. It heaved, spluttered, and off it went again as I hung onto the back for dear life. The boy laughed, pulling me back into the vehicle saying, 'do not worry, it is not the plane. In Cambodia nothing runs to time'.

My little friend was right. I was not the last to walk the plank onto what can only be described as a blue rusty-looking container, known as Boat Four. It did not surprise me that this sardine can, when it rolls over, leaves few survivors. Even a child would not have been able to climb through the tiny oval windows that ran along its length.

Inside the boat there were plush seats to the left and a pile of boxes and stools surrounding the boat driver to the right. The man at the entrance ripped my yellow ticket and, taking one look at my dusty state, pointed to the right of the boat, where a group of locals huddled. After climbing over food, bodies and bags of goodies, I squeezed myself into a corner, wedged between a Cambodian woman, six children and a smiling doctor. A chicken took a peck at my feet and a bag of rice exploded above my head, covering me and causing everybody else to laugh. Amused by my predicament, the doctor gave me a bag in which to collect the rice. Nothing is wasted in Cambodia. I tried to remove the worst of it and save as much as I could but days later I still found bits of rice in my shoes and parts of my gear. Indeed, one hotelier even asked me if I had recently married!

You could not believe any more people would fit into the small space but they just kept coming, pushing me nearer and nearer to the steering wheel and the only open window. It was sweltering, yet the sun was hardly up and I wished then that I had bought some water and snacks before leaving town. The Cambodians talked across me and smiled. Their faces had a surprising resemblance to the stone heads at Bayon, with a timeless inner calm; a peacefulness you rarely see in the hectic West. It was too hot to sit inside for long and with a five-hour journey ahead of us, I decided to forfeit my seat and clambered back over all the bodies, leaving the doctor to look after my belongings.

It was a good decision. The scenery was spectacular from the roof and as the boat picked up speed, I was cooled down by a much-needed breeze. The unfolding landscape was an added bonus as we passed houses on stilts with children laughing and playing in the water. Lots of pagodas, mosques and curiously shaped buildings dotted the landscape, popping out from behind bushes and trees. As we left the outskirts of Phnom Penh, the land became more sparse with only the occasional property in the distance.

Just when I was getting comfortable and had started to write my journal, there was a sudden loud bang and the boat stopped abruptly, almost throwing us off the roof into the muddy water below. We scrambled back, our bodies flat against the roof, worried that we had been the victims of some passing Khmer Rouge guerrilla crossfire. Only the week before the same boat had been hit by a round of ammunition and here we were in the heart of bandit country. Out on deck, with no real cover, we were sitting ducks. Smoke poured out of the front of the boat as it groaned, tipping in the other direction. The gears were wrenched again and more smoke billowed out onto the water as we recovered our original position and then everything went still – except for my heart which was thumping like mad. Had a stray bullet hit the fuel tank? What if we were taken captive? After seeing Tuol Sleng, I had no desire to be taken prisoner by the Khmer Rouge.

One of the boys lying next to me on the deck decided to sit up and survey the landscape, informing all of us pressed against the rusty roof that it was nothing to worry about, just the engine, which would be fixed within an hour. We sat floating in the middle of the water as the makeshift repairs were carried out. I felt scared as my life flashed before me, kicking myself for not having any water and wondering whether it was going to be a Western or Cambodian hour.

I was distracted from thoughts of starvation and bandit ambushes by a rather attractive Dutchman who appeared on deck. He entertained us with travel stories and recounted how he had read about the death of three French people in just such a situation only two weeks previously. This news quickly reinforced my view that my worst fears were not unfounded. According to the local English paper, the *Phnom Penh Post*,

Temples in the Jungle

the boats to Siem Reap were always encountering problems but then this was supposedly part of their charm. 'You miss all this if you fly everywhere', said the Dutchman, amused by my terrified expression.

Before any more horror stories could be recounted, the boat sped on, attempting to make up for lost time, passing women cleaning their clothes in the river and enjoying the wash of the speed boat. Like an electric washing machine, the swell cleaned the last of the soap suds off their clothes before they laid them out on the banks to dry in the sun. Being the rainy season it started to pour, forcing us to take refuge inside the boat. Back in the hold, a little girl had fallen asleep on my camera bag while her mother sat on my rucksack watching over her. So I stayed by the doorway looking out at the ominous thunder clouds and lightning flashes, relieved when the boat finally came into dock. Seven hours on the water had been more than enough for me.

With the number of people on the quay awaiting the boat's arrival, I wondered whether there was someone important on board. I soon discovered, as I disembarked, that it was Siem Reap's mafia of touts waiting to take visitors to their respective family guest houses. The taxi trip may be free but once you have selected to go with one of them, you are theirs for the rest of your stay at Angkor Wat.

In spite of the rain, I wanted to go and see the ruins as soon as possible and after negotiating with one of the hotel motorbike riders, off we went into the storm. En route to Angkor, I bought a US$40.00 three-day pass from the main tourist office, which enabled me to explore the site at my own pace. Flashing my pass at a group of men huddled together at the checkpoint, it took us less than twenty minutes to reach the main temple.

Angkor is the most frequently visited and written about ruin, although it is, in fact, only one of a thousand temples in the 120 square mile area. Many of the others have collapsed over time but thirty-nine of them are still accessible and, in most cases, extremely well preserved. Wiping the rain from my glasses, I got off the bike and waded through the water, up some grey sandstone steps to get my first view of the magnificent temple. As I looked at the incredible site set against the

Intrepid Journeys

dense, green undergrowth, I understood what the writer Jeanner de Beerski meant when he said: 'Go to Angkor, my friend, to its ruins and its dreams'. Arriving in the rainy season has its advantages – it lent the grey sandstone and red brick of the temples a magical, glistening light and through the torrential rain the blur of colour made it dreamlike.

The country once known as Nokor Kokthlok – the Country of the Island of Trees – has an irresistible appeal or, in my opinion, a fatal attraction. The reason being the ancient temple complex of Angkor, one of the Seven Wonders of the World. Angkor Wat is a temple city occupying some five hundred acres and has fascinated the outside world since its rediscovery in the last century.

Coming to Angkor from the West, it is easy to understand the passion it has inspired in writers past and present. Its artistic distinctiveness is as fine as that of the Taj Mahal and its beauty and stature can only be rivalled by the mighty Egyptian Pyramids and the pomposity of St. Peter's in Rome. As one walks down the main promenade, it is like stepping back in time to the era of the great temple builders. All around this magnificent complex is lush rainforest which has had to be hacked back to allow the temple, that was hidden for hundreds of years, to shine once again. For the people of Cambodia it is like a beacon of hope in the face of decades of ceaseless and pointless violence.

It is the centrepiece of one of the world's great religious empires, the Khmer, a Hindu-influenced civilisation that lasted six hundred years from 800 AD. The largest temple in the world, it took thirty years to complete, using as much stone as the Cheops pyramid in Egypt. Like the pyramids, Angkor Wat is believed to have been intended as a funeral temple for Khmer King Suryavarman II. Still in use – not just during festivals – pilgrims pay their respect by bringing gifts of fruit every day.

Angkor is particularly unusual because it faces west and is best at sunrise, contrary to the advice in guide books. Watching the sun rise over the three towers of Angkor, stylised in Cambodia's flag, is simply breathtaking. Find yourself a spot under a tree at the side of the main walkway if you want to savour the views in peace, away from the

Temples in the Jungle

commotion of the tourists. The towers appear like sleeping giants, turning from black to every shade of crimson, purple and orange. For the best view, head to the basin of water at the front of the temple and watch the brilliant colours spread across the sky, like a painter's palette reflecting back the most sensuous and startling aspect of this architectural masterpiece. As it is a practising place of worship one witnesses as many Hindus as tourists making pilgrimages to pay their respects to the gods.

Plans are under way to bring Angkor Wat alive with the old tourist favourite, a sound and light show, depicting its history. It is being billed as 'the biggest and best cultural event of its kind anywhere'. The show will not start until the end of 1999 so if you want to see the grandeur of the complex in the peace and serenity it was intended to be appreciated, hurry. But be careful as everything from mortar attacks to the deadly sniping Khmer Rouge make a visit to Cambodia a gamble.

The great temple walls surrounding Angkor are beautifully carved although slightly over-run by greenery. Despite the outlines being smothered in moss and ivy, it is still possible to pick out the bas reliefs depicting daily life. It is designed for viewing from left to right in accordance with Hindu funeral rituals but it also shows the mythology of the Hindu people.

With the decline of the Angkor period, the capital moved south and the area was gradually overrun by the jungle, disappearing under a green canopy of trees. For four hundred years it remained a myth to Westerners, until a Frenchman archeologist, Henri Mahout, stumbled across it by accident. You can get some sense of this by visiting Ta Phrom, a temple covered by huge writhing trunks of banyan trees that seem to slither like snakes across and around almost every stone in the complex. Passing through its narrow doorways, one feels as if one has entered the heart of a mighty jungle as cicadas, birds and monkeys fill the air with tropical sounds. The faces of the Angkor civilisation push their heads through the greenery and with their glassy stares seem to follow you as you explore its inner sanctum. This is the most adventurous of the temples and if one then visits Angkor Thom –

known as The Great City Featuring Two Hundred Huge Stone Faces – one may experience a sense of anti-climax.

The most fairytale of the Wats is Banteay Srei, the temple of women, noted for its delicate carving and pink colouring. Despite it being unsafe, a group of us decided to chance it and the visit certainly proved to be a truly unforgettable experience. Bullets were shot at us and although none of the party were hurt, we discovered afterwards that many other visitors had not been so fortunate.

It is worth remembering that although Cambodia may seem peaceful at times, it is always on the brink of violence. The Khmer Rouge continue to ship out and sell every log, gem and chipped-off Angkor statue it can get its hands on. Its many night raids make the area volatile and unpredictable. If you get in the way or they feel another spate of kidnapping would help their cause, that romantic midnight walk might just be your last. Always keep in mind the words of General Lon Nol, who led Cambodia to war: 'A people that could build Angkor could do anything'.

A Bus To Batad

by Mark Hodson

At the bus station in Baguio City, four hard-faced drivers sat huddled in a corner drinking beer. On the wall above their heads hung a sign that read, 'No sleeping on the tables'. A radio blared. Bruce Springsteen was singing *Born to Run*. It was 6.00am.

I had been in Baguio for less than twenty-four hours and was already anxious to get out. What foolishness! Baguio, according to the guide books, was known as the 'City of Flowers'. People who lived in the capital, Manila, raved about the place until tears of joy welled in their eyes. It was their summer capital, it was an oasis, a Shangri-la; it had parks, pine trees, cool mountain air, coffee bars and five universities. It was, sighed one taxi driver as he sailed through a set of red lights, known to some as the 'City of Lovers'.

The problem with Baguio was that it was altogether too European, both in its temperate climate and in the cool demeanour of its inhabitants. It also rained a lot. Personally, I had come to the Philippines in search of exotica – not a poorer version of Switzerland. Which was why I was heading further out into the mountains, looking for a bus to Sagada.

Intrepid Journeys

There is only one way to get to Sagada and that is along the Halsema Highway, a narrow unpaved road that penetrates deep into the heart of the central cordilleras. It climbs to over 7,000 feet above sea level and at some points is barely more than a dusty track carved into the side of the rock. It is so precipitous and winding, that the bus ride between Baguio and Sagada (distance on the map, sixty miles) takes a full eight hours. What is more, accidents on the road appear to be commonplace: according to an article in the Philippine *Daily Inquirer* only a few days previously, nine passengers had died and another eight had been injured when a minibus driver had taken a wrong turn down a 250 foot ravine. The use of the word highway was, possibly, ironic.

The bus was a creaking jalopy with wooden sides and hard seats. When we reached the first serious incline it slowed to a crawl and started spewing noxious black fumes. At the summit, the driver revved his engine as if in celebration, and we watched the sun rise over the distant peaks, dousing the rice terraces below us with a creamy warm light. Breathtaking though the scenery was, it had nothing on the driving. On the downhill stretches we screamed around hairpin bends on the wrong side of the road at buttock-clenching speeds. The driver was not a big fan of the brake pedal; his technique involved keeping a foot on the gas and a hand on the horn. Had he not he read the papers lately?

This was not my first encounter with dangerous driving in the Philippines. Indeed, I had probably witnessed more shunts, scrapes and heart-stopping near-misses here than anywhere else in Asia. This was especially alarming because the country is well known for its misfortune at the hands of natural disasters. Earthquakes, floods, volcanic eruptions and mudslides all seem to be routine occurrences in the Philippines. You might think, then, that people would get the message and drive more carefully. Not at all. Instead, they sell you insurance.

At the bus station in Manila, when I bought my ticket to Baguio, I was offered an insurance policy which would cover me against death or serious injury. For little more than twenty-five pence I could take my seat and relax in the knowledge that, should I fail to arrive in one piece, my family would be better off by several thousand pounds. Others may have found this reassuring – I did not. However, the odds seemed generous, so I paid up.

A Bus to Batad

If anything, as the terrain became more hazardous, so did the driving. Out on the Halsema Highway, far from the relative security of the capital, the prospect of rebel ambushes, earthquakes, falling rocks and killer hairpins would have made the idea of insurance ludicrous. Or, at least, ludicrously expensive. The compensation for putting your life on the line was purely aesthetic. In places the mountain scenery was so beautiful that passengers may have thought they had already died and gone to heaven.

By the time we reached Sagada my kidneys were aching with the constant bumping and jarring, and I was coated in a fine layer of dust. I emerged from the bus to find a lazy one-street town wedged in a low valley, surrounded by pine forests and lush terraces. I took a room at a cheap guest house and strolled across the road to a café that served homemade chocolate cake. After the relentless rattle and roar of the bus engine the town seemed eerily quiet.

This sense of calm and isolation lent Sagada more than a touch of the Shangri-las. But for all its bucolic charm, the town was in the heart of bandit country. Long-running hostilities between government troops and the communist New People's Army (NPA) had given the region a reputation for occasional and apparently random violence. The stakes were high – to the north of Sagada lay rich cannabis fields said to be controlled by the NPA.

After dinner I retired to one of the town's two bars where I was cornered by a local tourist guide with a scruffy coat and a manic toothless grin. He placed his beer next to mine and started telling me about a girl from New Zealand who had been involved in a road accident a couple of days previously. A bus from Banaue, the next town on my itinerary, had veered off the road and tumbled down the side of a mountain, he said.

'She is in the hospital here in Sagada. If you like, you can go and see her.'

'Is she badly hurt?'

'Oh yes', he replied, smiling and flashing his gums. 'She's dead.'

My thoughts turned quickly to escape and within seconds I was saved by the bell. It was 9.50pm, and the government curfew came into force in ten minutes. I did not even bother to finish my drink.

I woke at dawn to the sound of pigs squealing beneath my window and stumbled out of the guest house into brilliant sunshine where I was met by a boy aged about ten. 'Good morning', he said, 'you want to buy some hash?'

Behind him, a group of teenagers dressed in basketball shorts, bandanas and flip-flops were swaggering down the street. Each had an automatic rifle slung over his young shoulders.

'Are they rebels?' I asked the boy.

'No man, that's the army.'

★ ★ ★ ★ ★

To the few tourists who make it as far north as Sagada, the town is known for its so-called hanging coffins. They do not actually hang, but in keeping with the tradition of the local Igorot tribe, they are lodged high in the rock of the surrounding cliff faces so that they appear at first glance to be suspended in mid-air. The thinking behind this, I was told, was that it would enable the dead souls to find their way back to the earth's core.

An American man staying at my guest house said the coffins were only a mile or two out of town and were easy to find. He suggested I enlisted the help of a local guide, but after my encounter in the bar the previous evening, I opted to go alone.

After a cooked breakfast at the Shamrock Café, I wandered out of town past a line of thatched huts and corrugated steel houses. Men in tribal skirts squatted in the dust, sharpening long knives; women sold cakes and Coca-Cola from their doorsteps. I stopped several times to ask directions but the children giggled and ran away, and the adults just waved vaguely at the hills ahead. They did not give the impression of being overly friendly.

I was unsure what to make of these tribespeople. Back in Manila I had met two young English backpackers who claimed they had hiked for two days out of the nearby town of Bontoc in search of a 'lost tribe'. The tribe, they had been told, had little contact with Western civilisation. The terrain was difficult and the route unmarked but eventually they arrived at a village and were greeted with a warm welcome. The adults gawped and the children raced up to them, and

A Bus to Batad

clung to their arms. The two excited travellers were ushered into a hut and introduced to an old man who they took to be the village chief. He shook their hands and greeted them in English: 'Welcome, my friends. Please stay as long as you like. But first, we watch a video. You like Chuck Norris?'

After an hour of aimless wandering around the outskirts of Sagada I had almost reached the point of giving up. Then I looked up and saw them – groups of rough wooden coffins lodged in cracks and crevices high in the sheer rock face. I walked further and found more coffins, unmarked and dumped in unruly piles at the mouths of caves. Some had been prised open to reveal dusty skeletons draped in rags.

I came across a couple of Japanese tourists who, along with a local guide, were studying the grisly remains. The guide explained that some of the skeletons were headless because previous visitors had removed the skulls and taken them home as souvenirs. Despite the fact that the Igorot people had long since abandoned the practice of open-air burial, I was beginning to understand their coolness towards foreigners. The thought of well-heeled tourists casually raking through the bones of their ancestors must have been particularly galling.

★ ★ ★ ★ ★

The next trip was to Banaue, by jeepney, the ubiquitous and uniquely Filipino form of public transport on which virtually the whole country relies to get around. Each vehicle is a kaleidoscope of colour, festooned with religious icons, bull bars, mirrors, flags, flashing lights and cheerful slogans. Some of the older models started life as American troop carriers during the Second World War and newer versions had been built along similar lines: a bench seat along each side and an open back. They are low on comfort and high on social interaction, with your fellow passengers sometimes quite literally in your lap.

There were two jeepneys a day, one leaving at 6.00am, the other at 6.30am. I aimed for the early one, thinking that if I overslept I might have a chance of catching the second. When I arrived at the bus stand ten minutes early, the jeepney was almost full and ready to leave, its engine revving wildly.

We changed vehicles at nearby Bontoc where we had time for a breakfast of pancakes and coffee. Then we were off again into the mountains on rough roads, sometimes rising so high we were engulfed in mist. We stopped at army checkpoints twice, where young conscripts scrounged cigarettes from the driver and tried to look menacing. I asked a pair of them if I could take their photograph and as they posed for the camera their scowls broke into warm, ingenuous smiles.

Banaue is famous for its vast rice terraces, which have been dubbed – rather predictably – the eighth wonder of the world. They are an extraordinary sight. Rice terraces are not uncommon in Asia but at Banaue they are so extensive they cover an entire valley. It has taken the people of the local Ifugao tribe more than 2,000 years to build them, working step by step from the ground up, using only bare hands and primitive tools. Some rise as high as 3,000 feet, a testament to the power of the human spirit as much as the skill and ingenuity of the engineers.

There are said to be some 12,000 miles of clay and stone walls that support and enclose the paddy fields and which offer delightful, though treacherous, walking. The walls are only about twelve inches across and, each time you raise your eyes from the path to gaze at the awesome views, you run the risk of toppling into the squelching ankle-deep mud that lies on either side. After two days of exploring, both my feet had taken several soakings.

On my third day in Banaue I had just returned from a trek in the hills and was sitting at a café drinking tea when the earthquake struck. The first indication that something was wrong was a series of ripples that moved slowly across the surface of the tea cup. Before I had time to make sense of this, the cup had started to rattle in its saucer and the plate had slid several inches across the table top. Within a second or two, the table legs were hammering loudly on the wooden floor.

Nobody in the café said anything but there was a moment when the customers and staff all seemed to catch each others' eyes at once, as if waiting to be told the awful truth. Then, *en masse*, we kicked away our chairs and sprinted out on to the street, hearts pounding and pupils dilating.

There is something uniquely terrifying about being caught in an earthquake. It is not so much the thought that you might die, as the truly

A Bus to Batad

shocking news that absolutely nothing is safe any more. If even the ground we walk upon can crumble and give way, what then can we rely on? After an initial surge of adrenalin, victims are left with an overwhelming sense of dread and disorientation that strikes in the pit of the stomach.

The people of Banaue are no strangers to the kind of devastation that earthquakes can cause. Most had vivid memories of a major quake that had ripped through the region three years earlier and had measured 7.7 on the Richter Scale. It had claimed a total of 1,600 lives. This latest one was relatively small but as everyone in earthquake regions knows, small tremors are often followed by bigger ones.

Out on the street, there was no obvious structural damage. Some vegetables had rolled off a stall in the street and a few pictures had fallen from the walls of the café but the buildings looked unharmed. Several people around me were visibly shaken and a woman was sobbing and clutching a baby. One man appeared to be praying. Everybody, it seemed, was waiting for the next tremor.

Unsure of what to do, I returned to the café and shared a meal with another British backpacker. We talked about home, our families and friends, and then, as darkness fell, a loud rumble echoed across the valley. We froze, fearing the worst, then laughed like idiots when we realised it was only thunder.

It turned out we were staying at the same guest house, a three-storey concrete building suspended on wooden stilts above the side of the valley. My room was in the basement and as I was not in the mood for turning in for the night, we stayed at the café and drank beer – lots of it – whilst weighing up our options. Was it worth dragging our bedding out on to the street and sleeping under the stars, or would we be stripped and robbed by bandits? Before we could decide, the rain came. Giant globs of water clattered the roof of the café, so loud at times that we could barely hear each other speak. It was Biblical, end-of-the-world stuff. This was not a night for sleeping out.

At 1.00am the café closed and we ran through the rain to our guest house. I had a plan: a Heath Robinson-style early warning system. I took a couple of empty beer bottles, my alarm clock, a penknife and a pair of shoes and balanced each item around the room, as precariously as possible. I put them around the edges of tables, on the door handle and on the narrow window ledge, so that the slightest tremor would send them crashing to the floor, and me – fully dressed with all my valuables strapped to my waist – running out on to the street. I turned out the light and waited for sleep.

It was a long wait. At 5.30am I abandoned the idea of dozing off and started collecting my bits and pieces. It was a strange feeling, part relief and part disappointment. Out on the street people were already walking about. It was time to move on, so I packed my bag and squeezed on to a bus full of farmers, sacks of rice and a couple of noisy chickens and took a bumpy ten-mile ride higher out into the hills. The driver pulled up beside a steep footpath and pointed, 'This way Batad'.

I had it on good authority that Batad was an idyllic little village set amid rice terraces several miles from the nearest road. There were said to be a couple of guest houses with simple accommodation, some good walks in the area and nothing much else. It sounded like a fine place to unwind and forget about earthquakes.

It took me two hours to reach the summit of the hill, by which time I was soaked in sweat and wilting fast. The view, when I got there, was extraordinary. A patchwork of terraces stretched out over the valley floor and up the sides of the surrounding mountains like a huge green amphitheatre. It was stunningly beautiful and in the floor of the valley lay the village of Batad which consisted of no more than a couple of dozen traditional huts, one concrete house and a tiny church with a rusted tin roof.

There was a rustle in the bushes beside me and two small boys in bare feet and torn shirts appeared.

'Batad?' asked one.

'Yes.'

'Come. This way.'

I followed the boys down the hill, out of the undergrowth and into the rice fields. We walked along the tops of dry stone walls and through dusty back yards until we arrived at the concrete house where a cheerful woman in her forties called Christina showed me to my room.

'I hope you like it. You are the only guest right now', she said.

The room was simple but not uncomfortable. Although there was neither electricity nor running water, I had a double bed with a thick mattress: all the more remarkable given that everything in the village would have had to be carried from the road.

I sat on Christina's makeshift balcony, making small talk and watching the village children wash clothes on nearby rocks. Next door a wizened old woman with tattoos etched along the length of each arm tended to her chickens. Christina told me the tattoos had been applied by the woman's father when she had reached puberty so that she would be easy to identify, should she ever run away from the village. The chances of her running now looked slim.

Later in the afternoon three more guests arrived, accompanied by the barefoot boys, and Christina set about making dinner. When darkness descended, the palm trees were filled with fireflies and we ate rice and vegetables and drank bottles of beer. Christina's daughter, Vivienne, arrived home with her school friend and the two girls sang traditional songs and performed simple dances by the light of a kerosene lamp. As a concession to us, their repertoire included John Lennon's *Imagine* and Bryan Adams's *Everything I Do (I Do it for You)*. In gratitude, we bought them each a bottle of Coca-Cola. They could hardly have been more delighted had we offered them a recording contract and a six-figure advance.

I fell in quickly with the slow pace of life in Batad, and my intended overnight stay became two, three and then four days. Each morning I was woken at dawn by the rhythmic pounding of rice. It took an hour of strenuous activity to separate a handful of rice grains from the inedible husks, a task performed with a giant pestle and mortar. I managed it for ten minutes before my arms started to ache.

While the women worked up a sweat, pounding away with the pestle and mortar, the men seemed happy to spend their days drinking *tupuy*, a tear-jerking rice wine as strong as paint stripper. One morning, Christina's husband invited a few pals around for a drink in the hope of persuading them to do some heavy lifting. Nine hours later, at 6.00pm, they were legless and one man had to be hauled out of a shallow stream and carried home. It was hard to believe these were the same people who had built thousands of feet of rice terraces with their bare hands.

Behind the picturesque prettiness of Batad, all was not well in the village. In addition to the problem of drunkenness, heavy rain earlier in the year had damaged much of the rice crop and large sacks of rice had to be bought every week at the market in Banaue. Even low-spending tourists were welcomed for the little extra cash they injected into the crippled local economy.

Not everybody relied on rice to earn a living. One boy tried to sell me a block of dried cannabis leaves as big as a house brick, and others offered finely-worked wooden carvings of ancient Ifugao deities. I bought one which, I was told, was of Bulul, the rice god.

The Ifugao, like most of the Filipino people, were converted to Catholicism by Spanish missionaries in the sixteenth century. However, it was evident that strong traces of earlier pagan worship remained in Batad. In order to ward off evil spirits, the skulls of slaughtered pigs were nailed to the walls of houses, and stories were told of bloody vendettas and headhunts. Although disputes with neighbouring villages now rarely lead to violence, decapitation is still considered a legitimate form of redress. In 1977, a bus driver who ran over and killed a child was seized and summarily executed.

My last day in Batad was a Sunday. In the morning the villagers trooped into the church where they said some prayers for next year's rice crop and sang hymns with beautiful, soaring voices. I packed my bag, settled up with Christina and started out on the long walk back to the road. When I reached the top of the hill I turned to take a last look at the village below and watched the reflection of the sun inscribe glittering patterns on the rice paddies. I was exhausted from the climb, but I found that when I held my breath I could still hear the singing from the church, the voices drifting up on stray currents of warm air; part siren call, part momento.

Trouble On Paradise Island

by Anna Rockall

I had never jumped out of bed so quickly in my life. The blurry, sleepy realisation that I was about to be flame-grilled like a burger electrified me out of my middle-of-the night, half-drunk torpor and into action faster than a sprung jack-in-the-box.

You would have thought that someone would check if anyone was in when the hut next door caught fire and started burning in the fierce, unstoppable way bone-dry bamboo does. But, on the other hand, to the residents of Gili Trawangan – a tiny Indonesian island off of the bigger Indonesian island of Lombok, one down from Bali – who were faced with losing their livelihoods, one tourist more or less was probably irrelevant. Gili Trawangan may be a tropical paradise, an undeveloped coral-fringed island in the Java sea with pale gold and black volcanic beaches and the kind of arching palm trees so beloved of holiday brochure-makers; but its reisdents are not really big on fire drills.

Gili Trawangan is a tiny dot in the vast Indonesian archipelago, a mere three-and-a half square kilometres and home to only a few hundred. Despite being difficult to get to, it and its sister islands Gili Air and Gili Meno have become established stop-offs for travellers trying to escape the tourist madness of Bali. For the moment it is safe from real development because the only way to get there is in shallow-hulled motorboats that can make it over the coral reefs. The boats – some distant ancestor of the catamaran – crawl to the shore like huge insects, with four balancing wooden arms splayed out over each side to stop them tipping over when loaded down.

I caught one in Bangsal, a section of shore on Lombok which, by virtue of having a ticket office and a coffee shop, gets to call itself a harbour. When the boat pulled in, they crammed it with travellers, bags and provisions until the waterline lapped around the rim, and then we set off on the squashed and hair-raising journey to the island. The water sloshed along the bottom of the boat, soaking our belongings – particularly when we crossed the shallow, choppy waters over the reef – and we could only hope the boatman knew what he was doing. However, with some luck and skill combined, we crunched gently onto the beach with some relief an hour later.

Life on Gili Trawangan is a hammocked, sandy, languorous experience for the visitor. The evenings are a tropical lull of fresh fish and mosquitoes, shooting stars and sunburn. The days are a hazy headache of light, heat and inactivity, punctuated by dreamlike visits to the cooling coral underworld just a few metres away beneath the waves. I snorkelled as much to get away from the heat as to admire the coral; flying over a seascape of green brains and bottoms and limbs, forests with bright blue skeletal trees inhabited by parrot fish that changed colour in the shallow water, and angel fish with black and blue and yellow markings like a Picasso. There was a colossal grey and orange flat fish with a disconcerting array of teeth which I am sure I later saw displayed outside a restaurant.

With so much idyllic scenery around, it did not seem like anything could go wrong. I had been indulging myself on Gili Trawangan for nearly a week before disaster well and truly struck, The day of the fire

Trouble On Paradise Island

had been a bad day anyway. The bond amongst travellers, adrift in far-flung lands and drawn together by their common foreignness and shared interest in minor tropical diseases, is not as strong as one might hope. Trusting people simply because they speak the same language as you, or have travelled in a few of the same places as you, is a bad idea. But I was travelling alone for two months, and talking to all kinds of people is part of the whole experience. If I had not, I might well have gone mad with the solitude.

I had had a few drinks on the beach the evening before with a couple of Australians from Darwin – Murray and Nick – typical travellers trying to drink their way around Asia on a few dollars a day. We had had a meal of barbecued reef shark and then had lit a fire, looked at the silhouettes of palm leaves against the stars and marvelled at the bright sapphire sparks of phosphorous flashing in the waves – your average evening on a desert island. They were leaving early the next morning, so we said our goodbyes and retired to our respective huts.

It was not until lunchtime the next day, when I tried to pay for my *nasi goreng*, the standard meal of fried rice with anything else that happens to be around, that I realised that Nick or Murray must have pilfered through my bag while I was chatting to the other. They had nicked all my cash. The waiter was hovering around my table with a mixture of concern that he might not get paid and cynicism that my surprise and blustering excuses were just attempts to bludge a free meal. However, I could not magic the money out of nowhere, so after some argument he unwillingly accepted a spare T-shirt as payment.

My Australian friends had left me without a single penny. And as if that was not bad enough, I was due to set out the next morning for Jakarta for my flight home – an arduous journey across three islands on local transport which I had a few days to complete. One thing I certainly did not have was time to mess around. Now I did not have any money to get there either.

There are lots of wonderful things about Gili Trawangan – the limited transport to and from the island, the lack of telephones or

Intrepid Journeys

general electricity, the lack of police, the lack of banks, the ramshackle huts – all things which I had taken great pleasure in, but which now seemed to be conspiring against me. I still had my Visa card, so when I got to a bank it would be OK. The trouble was, the nearest bank was in Ampenan, an hour's bus ride away on mainland Lombok. That may not seem far but without money to pay for the transport, it might as well have been a million miles.

Without any phones, I could not call the airport in Jakarta to try and change my flight and give myself a little more time to sort out the mess I was in. I could not pay for the room I had been staying in, or for any more food or water. I could not even ask the boatmen if they might give me a free lift back to Lombok – not my favourite option considering how hard they worked for their pitiful living – because they would not be back on the island until the next day. And I did not even have the final option of every nice middle-class girl like myself; I could not call Mum for help.

The first issue was how to get off the island without paying for the boat. Short of swimming the shark-infested seas to Lombok, with all the attendant dangers of strong currents, jelly fish and sea snakes (not to mention my own gym-hating, over-indulging state of unfitness) I was stuck.

I entertained the possibility of not paying for the room, getting together the money for the boat, and then doing a runner. But there was no way I was going to rob a family that was so hard up, however desperate I was. I also wrestled with my conscience over stealing from another traveller. It would not have been difficult, security was lax on the island, and I would not have to clean my victim out in the way that I had been. I decided against it, being a well-brought up young lady, but I must shamefacedly admit that I kept it in mind as a last resort.

One thing was in my favour – to pay for my room, the boat ticket and a bus to Ampenan, I only had to raise the equivalent of about £15.00. However, convincing strangers to lend you that much, even if you truly intend to pay them back, is not easy – particularly on an island populated

Trouble On Paradise Island

solely by locals for whom it is a lot of money, and budget travellers who like to pretend it is a lot of money. I sat on the beach, tears welling up, and looked at the people lounging around sunbathing. The idea of asking them for money went against the grain. It was begging, and I could not bring myself to do that. Yet.

Selling something was the logical answer, if I could find anything in my festering pile of belongings that did not deserve to be burnt. A pair of well-worn sandals perhaps, with the strap half-broken. A selection of grubby T-shirts. A couple of well-thumbed books with the pages falling out, or some half-empty bottles of sun cream. The contents of a rucksack after you have been on the road for a while is not the most appetising collection of gear.

Then there was my camera. This was a decent piece of kit worth several hundred pounds. Even if I managed to find a buyer, I would probably only get a tenth of its value. I was torn. I did not want to see my beautiful camera, my pride and joy, go to some scabby traveller (I was in quite a mood by this time) for next to nothing. All that was left was the watch on my wrist – a shiny fake Gucci I had picked up in Singapore – and a pair of delicately scented trainers that had seen better days. I dried my tears and got to work.

Trawling the beaches in the beating midday sun, I soon realised that the other travellers were about as interested in buying a watch as they were in reading the telephone directory. They had all been turning down street salesmen offering them fakes of every make and style around Asia for months, so my pathetic offering did not impress them at all. And an island where time is measured by the space between drinks is not the best place to sell a watch. People were more keen to throw them away than to acquire them.

So, a little nervously, I tried out my sales technique on the locals. It was an odd turnaround, trying to sell goods to the Indonesians; it felt wrong trying to get money out of them when back home the poorest Westerner has more than they do. Like the rich girl in Pulp's song *Common People*, who pretends to be poor because she thinks it is cool, travellers play at being poverty-stricken, wearing shabby clothes and arguing over every penny, safe in the knowledge that they can stop it all and go home. Temporarily, I had less cash than the locals, but, even in my state of panic, I knew there was never really any question of my being stuck forever without the money to leave. Even if I did not make my flight, eventually I would get home safely. I would be bailed out in the end. The people I was trying to sell to did not have the luxury of being able to put a stop to the poverty.

The trainers were easy. Even in their dishevelled condition, they were stronger and more practical than what was locally available, and had the kudos of Western gear. I sat on the steps of the restaurant surrounded by a group of interested buyers – many of whom had no shoes at all – and tried my best to haggle the price up. The shoes passed from hand to hand, people tried them on, laughing over jokes I did not understand. I eventually convinced a young man sporting a drooping moustache and a serious expression to part with some cash.

The relief was huge. I had my ticket out of there. All I had to do now was get the money together to pay for my room. The watch was harder to sell. Shoes were practical but the watch was only useful as a trinket on Gili Trawangan. But isolated as they were, they did not get the chance to buy such things very often, and they all knew someone ('perhaps my brother, perhaps my cousin . . .') who might fork out their hard-earned money. Maybe I had been a street hawker in another life because within an hour one of the restaurant owners was the proud owner of a gleaming new watch and I was happily clutching a wedge of rupiahs. I collapsed on the beach and smugly watched the sun set over Lombok Strait, feeling unreasonably clever and resourceful. I felt like I had solved all my problems and was capable of anything. In fact, the real nightmare had not even started.

I went to bed early to make use of the one hour of electricity to try and pack, ready for an early start the next morning. The glow of the tiny flickering yellow bulb threw just enough light into the hut to make the shadows darker without making anything else lighter. I fumbled around

Trouble On Paradise Island

ineffectually for a while before giving up and trying to get some sleep in the sweat of the night. Lulled by the mysterious munching noises of something eating the hut – which had worried me at first but by now I had grown used to – I fell asleep.

When I woke up a couple of hours later and noticed a glow coming through the weave of the bamboo walls, I did not think much of it. I heard shouting on the street and did not think much of that either. There was a crackling noise. Sleepily I guessed there was a bonfire and someone was having a party. It took a few seconds to realise that no one would be dumb enough to have a bonfire on a street of bamboo huts in the dry season.

Panicking, I scrabbled out from under my mosquito net. The hut was in darkness and my belongings were scattered everywhere. I grabbed the sarong I used to cover the bare pillow and wrapped it around me. The crackling intensified; the roof of palm leaves over my head had caught. Real fear set in. There was no time to think. My money belt was under the pillow. I snatched it and ran out of the hut. Somehow, despite the confusion, I still managed to think how dramatic I must have looked, emerging from a flaming hut.

The scene outside was pandemonium. People were running towards the burning huts from all directions, shouting. Some were wailing, some were trying to throw buckets of sea water onto the fire, which was spreading fast. They might as well have spat on it for all the good it did. I was bumped and hustled as I tried to retreat uselessly from the heat, which had in a matter of seconds grown intense.

The hut where it had started – probably by a candle left unattended, or dodgy wiring – was already nearly destroyed. My hut was beyond saving. Less than a minute after I had woken up, the fragile palm roof collapsed in flames over the bed where I had been sleeping. I winced. These two huts were destroyed and it was clear the whole row was in danger. A group of men, frantic to save what was left of their livelihood, risked the flames and the heat, and grouped around the side of my hut. Straining with their backs against the raised floor – which was, like all of them, on stilts – they pushed what was left of the structure onto the remains of the first hut in attempt to control the fire. It was brave, it was the only chance they had, and it did not work. The next hut along caught.

The sky was glowing with the light from the fire and more and more people were arriving to see what was happening. I stood on the beach out of harm's way with the rest of the tourists, most of whom had been at a party further down, and we watched the flickering reflection in the waves as the village was destroyed. The fire swept along the row of huts lining the street to the sea, and then along the road down the beach. Then it turned as if it was not quite done yet, and burnt down the back row of huts.

There was nothing to be done and within a few hours it was all over. The embers of the village blinked out gradually, leaving only the black soot blown around by the wind until everything was covered. One restaurant at the end of the beach was still standing, so at the owner's invitation we all huddled in uncomfortably and tried to get some sleep on the floor, haunted by anything that sounded like it could be the fire starting up again.

The villagers had lost about twenty-five huts but with the panic of the sweeping flames behind them, they seemed calm. No one had been hurt – though I did wonder if anyone had checked, seeing how close I had come to being toast myself. It would take some time and effort to rebuild the huts but it could be done. The lost income would make it a struggle, but their attitude was that they would have to manage. Their fortitude and practicality was admirable. They all pulled together and the next morning they started clearing up and looking for new building materials.

Other travellers had lost their luggage but because most had been out at the time it started, they had their valuables on them. I had managed to get my money belt, which contained my passport, tickets and credit card. But the money I had gathered together so desperately the day before had been in the pocket of my shorts, which had been duly

Trouble On Paradise Island

cremated along with all my other possessions. To top it all, the only clothing I had was a semi-see-through sarong with no shoes and no underwear. I kept thinking, if this was a 1970s adventure movie, I would be one of those heroines who loses all her clothes in the second scene and struggles through the jungle for a week barely-clad but with perfect make-up at all times. All I needed was a hero to rescue me.

Again, I had no money and still no time to spare, but now I had no clothes either. It was so awful it was funny. I also had nothing to sell. My beautiful camera that I had resisted selling the day before was a molten piece of plastic, melded forever to Indonesian soil. The qualms I had had about begging or asking for help disappeared like smoke – I certainly was not going to travel across three islands to Jakarta all but naked.

The travellers who had been so unwilling to help me out by buying my shabby wares were wonderful. I asked around and managed to get a pair of shorts, a T-shirt and some sandals, despite the fact that several of the people I approached had lost all but what they we wearing. I may have looked ridiculous in shoes two sizes too big, a pair of boxer shorts and a T-shirt adorned with the words, 'Where the f**k is Lombok?' but I felt so well-equipped it made me wonder why I had needed so much gear before.

I swallowed my pride and asked for money, too. I raised just about enough, effusively thanking my benefactors and blushing as this was the first time I had ever accepted charity. It was a strange morning on the beach, with the ashes of the fire all around, the Indonesians hard at work putting their lives back together, and me wandering around begging while we waited for the boats to arrive. When I finally got on board I was so happy I nearly kissed the boatman.

Well, of course I made it back in one piece – and I have never begged since. From what I hear, Gili Trawangan has picked up the pieces and now has a thriving tourist industry that is far more sophisticated than the ramshackle set-up I left behind. I was pleased to see that a well-known guide book even carries a reference to the fire, with a stern warning to visitors to please be a little more careful with their candles.

Fortunately for Gili Trawangan, and tragically for Sumatra, the vast forest fires that have been raging in Indonesia over the last couple of years have not made it as far east as the island, and the devastation that is blighting large tracts of the rest of the country makes my own little experience seem match-sized in comparison. In some places, the fires have made clouds that have blocked out the sun for days, and the shrinking of the rain forest is having devastating repercussions for humans, wildlife, and the planet. So when you go to Indonesia, if there is anything left, please be careful with your candles.

Going Naked At The Mela

by Steve Davey

As soon as I heard about it, I just knew I had to go. In a land of excesses and superlatives, this was the big one. A religious event of such proportions that it was expected to attract between ten and fifteen million people on the most auspicious day, 14 April, to bathe in the Ganges. The last Kumbh Mela was three years ago and there would not be another one until the new millennium. The mela at Allahabad, nine years ago, had been the largest single gathering of people on the planet. How could I stay away?

After an arduous bus journey from Delhi, we were dropped a few kilometres out of Haridwar in a temporary station that looked like a storage area for livestock. Indian festivals are a lesson in crowd management. In the past thousands of people have been crushed to death at the Kumbh Mela – most notably in the 1950s when two rival groups of Sadhus (holy men) clashed and an elephant used in a procession stampeded. To prevent this happening, the whole town had been pedestrianised. Order was kept by scores of policemen, often in full riot gear, armed with the infamous *laathis* (long bamboo cane sticks) and each gripping a shrill whistle in his mouth.

Intrepid Journeys

The only legal way to enter town was to walk but we managed to find a couple of cycle *rickshaw-wallahs* who knew a back route and were prepared to break the rules. We haggled a price and set off. After a few hundred metres we swung off the main road and cut through small lanes and backstreets at a furious pace, rocking from side to side and lurching dangerously at every corner. We rejoined the main street just opposite the railway station and some twenty yards from our hotel. Two policemen waved their *laathis* at our *rickshaw-wallahs* and whistled furiously.

Our unceremonious arrival culminated in a mad scramble from the rickshaws, quickly paying off the drivers and dashing up the road, the whistles still ringing in our ears. It was here that we learnt a vital lesson which we were to exploit later. The police appeared to have orders not to leave their posts and so could not chase anyone past the nearest roadblock.

As befits its religious status, Haridwar is both vegetarian and 'dry'. A prominent notice in the foyer of the hotel stated it was illegal to even own alcohol in the town, let alone drink it. Our room overlooked the main road and we sat for a couple of hours acclimatising ourselves before heading out to explore the town.

The days leading up to the Kumbh Parva, the main bathing day of the festival, passed remarkably peacefully and we soon drifted into a pleasant routine of strolling round the festival and the huge encampments of Sadhus, and indulging in leisurely meals. Most evenings we climbed up to a small plateau on the hillside which towered behind the main Har Ki Pauri Ghat, crowned by the Mansa Devi Temple. This ghat is considered the precise spot where the Ganges leaves the sacred Himalayan mountains and where bathers congregate to wash away their sins.

The plateau has a commanding view over the ghat and was being used by India Radio for its live broadcasting. In between programmes, journalists and photographers were allowed to share the view. The ghat is centred on a canal, which diverts off the main tributary of the river. A recent man-made island forms one side of the canal and a series of bridges link it to the far side of the river and the original ghat to the west of the river. These bridges form the basis of the one-way system used to channel the pilgrims to, and away from, the ghat. I was expecting the Har Ki Pauri Ghat to look older and more spiritual, but apart from a sprinkling of temples and an old clocktower which loomed incongruously over the island, it looked like a series of art-deco pedestrian intersections painted bright creamy-yellow and garish terracotta. The ghat has been extensively expanded over the years to cope with the huge numbers of pilgrims but with all the skill and tact of 1970s town planners.

At this point the current is so strong that a great iron chain has been slung parallel to the bank to prevent the pilgrims being pushed into the water by the crowds and swept away. Similar chains hang from the bridges to give anyone in the water one last chance at salvation before the river carries them away.

During the festival, the priests at Har Ki Pauri performed the *Ganga aarti* prayers at sunset every evening. To the accompaniment of chants from the crowd, prayers from the priests and a great clashing of cymbols, flaming lamps were brought from the temple and offered to the Ganges. The pools of warm light illuminated a scene of timeless religious fervour as the pilgrims struggled to wave their hands through the flames to receive a blessing.

One day we decided to walk across one of the tributaries towards a sprawling campsite and fairground complex which crouched like a refugee settlement in the distance. Initially the path ran along a dry, stony river bed, with stalls selling souvenirs on either side. Interspersed in-between, all manner of beggars and cripples were plying their older trade; holding out leprous stumps and wailing pitiful impeachments at the passing pilgrims.

The path led to a long, low pontoon bridge, which crossed the slow moving water. On the far bank a few pilgrims were bathing in a half-hearted manner. On the stony beach leading up to the far bank was a small shelter. Covered by blue tarpaulin and open on three sides, it looked out over the river towards Har Ki Pauri Ghat. A ring of Indians were sitting cross-legged in front of the shelter, looking in at a skinny brown man, naked except for his long, matted dreadlocks.

Squinting against the setting sun he fixed us with a fearsomely mischievous look and, raising himself slightly from his sitting position, beckoned to us with an imperious wave of his left arm. We wandered over and sat down to the left of his retinue. He beamed at us proudly and then broke into a chesty, hacking cough, which doubled him over. His dreadlocks easily reached the ground as he slouched cross-legged on a rug. He had a long, straggly black beard and red-ringed eyes, no doubt a result of the large reefer he was holding in his right hand. Every few seconds he cupped his hands and inhaled deeply from this, quite literally, hand-made pipe, holding his breath until it shot out in a paroxysm of coughing.

His skinny body was a luxuriant brown, lightly dusted in ash from the fire that stood in a temporary hearth at his feet. His beaming, stoned smile was the perfect complement to his gratuitous nakedness, as he looked expectantly at K and me. I do not know if he expected us to be shocked but I could feel the pressure on my right arm as K, just out of frame, her view obscured by a bare skinny thigh, leant over to try to subtly get a better view.

Two of the retinue introduced themselves as teachers - particularly verbose teachers. They translated as they were the only ones who spoke English – very precise, sing-song English, interspersed with the rhetorical questions that typify Indian bureaucracy. He leant towards me and began his monologue: 'This man, his name is Baba Bhagwan Giri. He is a naga Sadhu. Do you know what a naga Sadhu is? A naga Sadhu is a holy man who walks around naked. Do you know why he is walking around naked? He is walking around naked to show that he is not needing any material possessions. That is making him an ascetic. He is a special, holy man. Not like us mere mortals. He is travelling here for the mela. Every day he is coming to bathe. The rest of his good time he is just sitting here and praying and thinking.'

Suitably introduced, the Baba welcomed us with a *namaste* (the palms - together greeting typical of India). In slow, vague Hindi, he told me the story of the mela, patiently waiting for the schoolteacher to translate and embellish his words.

As with most things in India, the Kumbh Mela is complicated and bureaucratic. It is held every three years in four different locations – Ujjain, Nasik, Haridwar, and Allahabad (Prayag) – in rotation. Its origins are in Hindu mythology. Apparently the gods and the demons churned an ocean of milk to extract an elixir of immortality which they stored in a large pot or *kumbh*. Although the gods agreed to share this with the demons, they stole

Going Naked At The Mela

it away and a great chase ensued. The chase lasted twelve days and during this time four drops of the elixir or *amrit* were dropped in the four places which now hold the mela. A god day lasts as long as a human year, hence the twelve year cycle of the Kumbh Mela.

For the devout Hindu, bathing at one of these locations is considered to wash away mortal sins, freeing the pilgrim from the cycle of rebirth. On the special days of the Kumbh Mela these sites are considered particularly auspicious and pilgrims travel from all over India in an unequalled display of faith. The actual dates of the mela are fixed by the stars and the lunar calender, when Jupiter is in Aquarius and the sun enters Aries. Astrologers and mystics gather together to predict not only when it should take place but also which the special days will be. The definitions are loose enough to allow for much debate and argument – especially amongst the various Sadhu factions. Once the dates of the mela are fixed, the state government apparatus moves in. The cities which hold the mela are in three different states and there is a great deal of local rivalry. The pressure is on to hold the 'best' and safest mela. A great deal of money is also allocated to public works.

As the Baba was speaking, an acolyte was making us tea over the open hearth. K and I regarded the murky brown liquid in the small dirty glasses with great suspicion but sipped it gingerly out of politeness. Cloyingly sweet and milky yet infused with a smoky tang from the fire it was refreshing, but I did wonder what havoc it might wreak.

I asked the Baba if I could take his photograph. He nodded his assent and sat up painfully straight. He ran a hand through his long dreadlocks in an attempt to prepare himself and stared down the camera. After I had finished he beckoned for the camera and proceeded to shoot half a film on a sweeping panorama of his followers who sat round him. He cackled in delight every time the motor whirred and advanced the film, ready for another exposure.

The numbers of pilgrims walking round the town and bathing in the river seemed to grow daily, and when, on the eve of the Kumbh Parva, we again went to watch the *Ganga aarti* prayers, it had swelled in size and fervour to biblical proportions. The island and the ghats were thronged with people and the marshalling area on the far bank was packed. In the dark blue light of the dusk we could barely make out the people but the restlessly expectant murmur never ceased to rise and fall with the wind. Once the prayers had finished the bathing would continue throughout the night.

We watched for a few hours and then hurried back through town for a rendezvous with some other tourists at a restaurant near the hotel. In its dimly lit and over-airconditioned interior (in India the cost and supposed quality of the food goes up in direct and inverse proportion to the temperature and wattage of the light fittings) we ate a mediocre meal in a state of high excitement whilst planning how we would negotiate the roadblocks which had sprung up all over town.

We were going to pretend to be a bizarre news reporting team. Gus and Rhys, two sound recordists making a record of the mela were going to flaunt their big, fluffy directional microphone, K and I were going to wave my cameras, and Carol (the sister of an old friend from London who happened to be on our plane to Delhi) and her friend were going to tag along and try hard not to look like hippies. Hopefully we could bluff our way past, despite our lack of official press passes. In true Indian bureaucratic fashion these had already run out.

Should we not get past the road blocks, we would have to take a detour to other side of the river via a roadbridge, through the miles of wooden fenced pens set up to channel pilgrims on the far bank, across the footbridges to the main ghat and out the other side to the alleyway which led to our intended vantage point. This would take hours and we would miss the processions of the naga Sadhus who were to lead the bathing.

The plan seemed foolproof that night but as we set out from the hotel at 5.00am into streets already thronged with people, it seemed rather ambitious. At the first main roadblock we were turned back and so followed some locals across a dry and stinking river bed which had been used as a sewer/latrine for the whole mela. From here we ducked blindly through a series of narrow backstreets until we came to a main road which led through the maze of streets used for the Bara Bazaar (Big Market). Each time we came to a police roadblock we attempted to talk our way through but on most occasions we had whistles blown in our faces and were sent back.

Going Naked At The Mela

Eventually, however, with a combination of diplomacy and bravado we pushed our way through and after climbing over a low wall made it to a point just opposite our goal.

In a mad dash we ran across the main ghat road and ducked into the alleyway with the sound of police whistles shrilling after us. It had taken us over an hour to make the journey and the sun was beginning to rise as we took our places on the plateau overlooking the ghat.

The view was breathtaking. Every inch of available space on the ghat, the bridges and the far bank was full of people making their way to bathe. A number of lesser ghats stretched down the banks of the river, and it was only with the benefit of the overview offered by India Radio that we could fully appreciate the size of the mela. The part which was centred on the town of Haridwar and Har Ki Pauri Ghat was only a fraction of the whole complex. Vast tented camps had been erected by the state authorities and people were bathing on both banks of the river as far as the eye could see. Above the drone of voices floated the sound of a thousand whistles as the police inarticulately directed the crowds. This sound more than anything typified the mela for me. It carried on day and night, more or less, for the duration of my time in Haridwar.

At around 7.00am the flow of pilgrims was stopped at the far bank and the bridges from the far side of the river gradually emptied. Two bridges allowed people over to each side of the ghat. Those on the island exited on a third bridge back across the river whilst those on the original ghat left through the town and back along the main road.

Some sixteen *akharas* (sects) of Sadhus were at the mela, and they were all to proceed to the ghat to bathe. The processions were traditionally led by the naga Sadhus. These were ascetic and militant orders, trained in martial arts who were formed to protect their religion from the Muslims during the Mogul era. As naga Sadhus they are supposed to eschew all material possessions and some of the more extreme orders, such as the Juna Sadhus, take this to extremes. They are reputed to cover themselves with ash from cremation pyres and undertake bizarre rituals which are said to involve eating such things as human excrement and human flesh.

There is always a dispute over which of the *akharas* will march first in

Intrepid Journeys

the procession. At Chaitra Amavasya bathing day the month before, the Juna and Niranjani *akharas* clashed, resulting in a couple of deaths.

The authorities were not taking any chances this time and rumours were flying. The mornings papers were already screaming that the whole procession had been cancelled as a summit meeting of Sadhus had failed to reach an agreement and that riot police had been mobilised to keep the Juna *akhara* from marching. They would have a hard job as there were said to be over 2,000 Juna at the mela and they are not known for their willingness to bow to authority. The good broadcasters at India Radio were convinced that the processions would happen but they would be late. A high-ranking policeman believed that the processions would not be happening and, rather optimistically, that the 300 police mobilised against them would keep them from leaving the camp.

Some time after the procession was due to begin, the crowd on the far side of the river stirred with excitement. A long column of naked Sadhus came into view from behind a row of trees. They made slow and stately progress - no one would try to hurry nagas. As the procession crossed the middle footbridge an Indian journalist told me that they were not the Juna but the Naranjani. There were hundreds of Sadhus in the procession - most of them naked. Sprinkled amidst them were the Gurus, or teachers. They walked under ornate umbrellas to shield themselves from the sun and were often protected from the crush by a circle of hand- or rope- holding peons.

The nagas lined up on the steps of the original ghat and then jumped *en masse* into the Ganges. Hinduism tends to be a fairly euphoric religion compared to its more solemn alternatives and the Sadhus were living up to this, laughing and splashing each other with wild abandon. When they finished washing away their sins they assembled on the bridge leading back across the river and began their procession to their camp.

On the opposite bank the Mahanirwani *akhara* procession was held up by the tail end of the next column of Sadhus from the Naranjani *akhara*. It looked like another battle might ensue but after much shouting of insults and threatening gestures, the Sadhus parted.

The processions continued all morning, and as the more benign, clothed orders reached the river they all seemed to merge into one melange of colour. I later learnt that late the previous night agreement on the marching order had been reached but the that Juna *akhara* had deemed that as they had not been given enough notice, had refused to march. This was in part caused by the perceived insult and in part by a ban on the carrying of their traditional weapons.

They were apparently still back at their camp in the middle of town, and I decided to go and see what was happening. I joined the crowds on the main ghat road and slowly made my way past the line of beggars towards the Juna *akhara*. One beggar was dressed as a Sadhu but his left arm and a good part of his shoulder was missing. Another had no legs and sat patiently on a wheeled wooden platform with his begging tin on the ground in front of him. Indian festivals attract beggars from almost as far as they attract pilgrims and the line reached some 200 metres up the road.

In the past the Juna camp was completely out of bounds. Few people were allowed in and those that were, were not made particularly welcome. In 'No Full Stops in India', Mark Tully, writing about the 1989 mela at Allahabad, paints them a fearsome reputation. However, things have changed drastically in the ensuing years and the Juna camp at the Haridwar mela was being treated like a fairground as pilgrims and a smattering of tourists walked and stared at the nagas in their tented pavilions.

Some of the Sadhus did look like genuine mystics and were meditating or performing feats of yoga but many of them were lounging around and even watching television. In the back of one tent I saw a Sadhu with thin, wasted legs standing up with the aid of a swing. He had apparently been standing up in this way for years as a way of concentrating his mind on his prayer. He was smoking a large reefer and watching a televised Hindi drama.

A small and skinny man dressed as a Sadhu came up to us and invited us to his pavilion. As we walked in we were confronted by the comatose bodies of three Dutch tourists who were too stoned to move. The Sadhu made a joke at their expense to his garrulous friends who were sitting at the far side of the tent, and then proceeded to watch an American documentary on alligators whilst we were served tea. After we had drunk the tea he asked for a huge donation and suggested we take the Dutch with us as they were making the place look untidy.

The Kumbh Mela is renowned for being one of the greatest gatherings of Sadhus in India and I had been particularly looking forward to seeing the nagas. I came away from the Juna *akhara* disappointed. Far from renouncing material possessions they appeared to have surrounded themselves with them. The comfort of their camp seemed, in some way, to have betrayed the millions of people who had given up so much and endured such degrees of hardship to be there; who, even now, were living in conditions which, by sheer weight of numbers and despite the best intentions of the authorities, resembled refugee camps. As the remorseless march of feudally religious India towards the twenty-first century continued, I was left wondering how long the Kumbh Mela, as an institution, will last on this scale. For all their star-billing this has nothing to do with the Sadhus or the organisers of the religion. The Kumbh Mela is about the pilgrims whose faith leads them time after time to follow in the footsteps of their gods without demurring to expense or hardship. Their self-sacrifice and quiet, modest faith impressed me far more than that of the Sadhus. They were the mela and its future lay with them.

That evening we walked down the banks of the Ganges. Everything was surprisingly subdued. Most of the pilgrims had gone back to the network of tented camps and only a relative few were still in the central area. Fewer still were bathing in the icy water. Those that were ducked hurriedly in the water, whilst still hanging onto to the rusty chain intended to stop them from being swept away. A wave of peace had washed over the mela ground. There were a couple more big bathing days, but the main one had passed, remarkably, without serious incident.

We bought a couple of small bowls made of leaves and containing a few grains of *prasad* (puffed rice) and a candle wick sticking out of some *ghee* (oil) as an offering to the *Ganga*. The flames fluttered precariously as we gently lowered the bowls onto the swirling waters. They were grasped away by the current and twirled around one another as they disappeared into the black, all consuming waters of Ganges.

Taking The Trunk Road

Lyn Hughes

The dapper-looking bespectacled man looked for all the world like a company director. He stepped forward and presented me with a hand to shake, and a garland for my neck. 'Welcome', he said as we exchanged business cards. 'Village Headman', I read. Things in the hilltribe areas of Thailand have certainly changed in the last decade.

I had been trekking in the north of Thailand many years ago but this time I would be doing it on four legs rather than two – I was going on elephant back. I have fond memories of seeing a wild elephant all those years ago, but now, as elsewhere in Asia, this population has dwindled rapidly and there is believed to be less than 2,500 elephants left in Thailand. Furthermore, many thousands of elephants used to be domesticated but now that logging is officially banned in Thailand, the number of working elephants has fallen to less than 2,000.

Stories vary as to the plight of the redundant elephants. Some are being used by illegal loggers; some have been left to starve; some are supposedly begging for food in the streets of Bangkok. Others have ended up in the various 'elephant camps' that now offer rides to tourists, and these may help to conserve their future. But I was to go a step further and spend a week in the close company of one.

The rendezvous point was near Mae Hong Son, by the Burmese border. I was swiftly introduced to the rest of my entourage, a bottle of water was thrust into my hands, and we headed off the track to where my elephant awaited. From a distance he did not look particularly tall but once I was asked to mount he seemed massive, despite having descended to his knees. I had hoped that we would have been introduced but we seemed to be in a hurry to head off. I was chivvied on, and rather ungracefully managed to land on the elephant's head facing the wrong way.

I had had visions of just me and an elephant riding off into the sunset together but this was to be a real team effort. I had my personal guide, Meo (pronounced 'maiow' – as in the noise cats make), a vivacious and charming lady from Bangkok. Then there was the *mahout*, Paluepor, his brother, Takewa, and a local guide KT. All were from the Karen village of the headman I had met. We also had a coordinator, Jak, and a porter, along with a pony with no name.

It transpired that Meo had never been trekking before. Looking distinctly glamourous in her white pumps and stylish sunglasses, I wondered how she would fare. However, within twenty-four hours she was skipping up and down the hillsides with no problem, growing increasingly adept at springing onto the elephant. As the days passed she graduated to launching herself on board via trees and rocks.

Our elephant was called Paserdor, and was fifty years old – just middle-age for elephants, who can live past eighty. He had spent most of his life working in the forests, carrying felled trees, but was now used for tourist rides in Mae Hong Son. He had no tusks. They had been removed when he was young to discourage poachers. Paluepor, explained that he belonged to somebody in Chiang Mai who leased him out. I was struggling with the pronunciation of his name, so decided to christen him Pat.

Taking The Trunk Road

Paluepor coaxed him along, using his feet and a soft voice. He carried a bamboo stick but this was only to swat flies. Having been upset in the past by the over-use of the spiked metal *ankush* used by Indian *mahouts*, it was encouraging to see Paserdor doing all that was asked without any use of force. Within a few hundred yards of us moving off I began to appreciate that we would be travelling at a pace dictated by the elephant.

Initially the track was broad and flat and the pace regular. However, we soon came to our first hill, short but steep, which I was surprised we were going to climb. However, Pat continued, slowly but surely, sometimes using his trunk to balance. If the climb up had been easier than I expected, the equally steep decline was to be more challenging – for myself and Meo, if not for the elephant. As Pat started to descend the feeling was rather like coming over the crest of a funfair rollercoaster, and I felt that same sinking feeling in the pit of my stomach that one feels when there is nothing in front of you.

It was a hot afternoon and Pat stopped at every stream and river. It was the dry season so the water levels were low, but Pat drew up the muddy water in his trunk and sprayed himself – and sometimes me – in order to cool down.

We were to spend the first night in a hilltribe village, home to fifty families of the Red Lahu tribe, and after three hours trekking we arrived. It is impossible to enter a village unobtrusively when mounted on an elephant, and I felt a tad self-conscious as we squeezed in amongst the houses. The majority were wooden, and built in traditional style on stilts. Pigs and chickens foraged and sheltered below, snuffling around for any peelings or leftovers that had been pushed through the floor. Pat soon had a following of the village children, like a large grey Pied Piper.

The first surprise was the lack of traditional costume. 'I can arrange some people to wear traditional costume if you want', said Jak. 'But that would be like Hollywood', I declined. The second surprise was the modern houses being constructed. One in particular stood out. Although built in wood, it had dispensed with stilts, and looked for all the world like a two-storey Alpine chalet. It belonged to a former trekking guide, who had now switched to the less physically arduous task of selling satellite dishes. When Meo saw how startled I was at the progress in the village, she commented: 'I dream that every village will be like a European village – with electricity and water. Then the tourists will come for the beautiful scenery, not to look at the people'.

We were to stay in a room that doubled as a shop, and had a large 'window' which was used as the counter. Thirty or so children soon appeared. They perched on a wooden bench outside the window, and peered in as Meo and I arranged our gear and set up home in a corner.

Dinner was cooked on a fire out on the verandah: a green curry, an omelette and stir-fried vegetables. Some women then tentatively made their way into our room and sat down, staring at us and chatting amongst themselves. Gradually the room filled with children in traditional costume of sequinned tops and long skirts, and after a few prods and encouraging smiles from their mothers, they sang and danced.

When they left we settled down but it was difficult to sleep with the shuffling and snuffling of the animals below the floor, the creaking of the hut and the barking of dogs. I was woken very early the next morning by the sounds of roosters crowing, and then became aware of the rhythmic echoing thud of rice being milled. I got up and made my way to the source of the sound. A woman and her two daughters smiled as they took it in turns to use their weight to send the wooden contraption up and down. I had had a go myself the previous evening and knew just how strenuous it was.

School did not start until 10.00am and the village children were either helping with chores or busy playing. Behind the hut in which I had slept, a homemade see-saw had been improvised by balancing a plank of wood over a log and three small children were giggling as they swung up and down. A few small boys were running up and down the narrow 'streets', propelling inner tubes with sticks. Over at the schoolhouse a few children were already arriving, although lessons were not to start for an hour or so. A few girls were in a cooking compound

Taking The Trunk Road

preparing a lunchtime stew – the pupils bring their own bowl of rice from home to accompany it.

Paluepor rode up on Pat, and he and Takewa started to 'tack up' as a crowd of children gathered to watch. Several layers of matting made from the bark of what was called the 'red tree' were laid on first. This was followed by a thick bamboo mat, and finally a wooden *howdah*, topped with a couple of cushions.

Setting out, we passed into Karen territory and through a mixture of cultivated land and bamboo forest. Takewa pointed out the various fruits and trees, both cultivated and wild. Meo soon dubbed him 'Uncle', a sign of respect. As the day grew hotter he picked and passed around a small sour fruit. A natural thirst-quencher that was picked with glee by everyone but me when spotted.

I had decided to walk but slipped a couple of times on the steep tracks, smothered by fallen leaves. Uncle cut me a walking stick from bamboo: 'To support your weight', Meo translated. All hopes of an Indiana Jones image had been blown, but my pride recovered when Meo and Uncle started using sticks too. The pole really proved its worth when we came to a river and, following it, crossed and recrossed, using our sticks to balance on the stepping stones. Here in the cool shade, birds sang and frogs plopped into the water as we made our way along. Butterflies, large and small, flitted along the banks, and the shallows were thick with tadpoles.

We caught up with the others in a small clearing and stopped for a leisurely lunch, and Uncle demonstrated the versatility of the surrounding bamboo, boiling the water for our tea in it, while cutting sections from it to use as cups.

Desperate to bond with the elephant I kept taking it little treats from my lunch; bananas, melon and watermelon. I would place them on his thick tongue and he would gently take them – but would then stare impassively at me, before going back to the serious business of devouring the nearest tree.

In the afternoon I decided to mount Pat again, and we carried on through the forest, past a grove that had once housed a monastery, and where trees are protected by saffron lengths of material. The previous day I had found myself chafing at the slow speed of the elephant but I had now adjusted and found myself lulled by the gentle, swaying motion. On his back I was conscious of having a totally different perspective, being at the same height as the lower branches, rather than walking underneath them. Birds sang at my level, fruit could be plucked with ease and flowering orchids grew out of the tree trunks, providing a vivid splash of colour.

We finally broke out of the woods into a long valley, farmed by Karen people. There was little cultivation at this time of year but buffalo and cattle roamed free, and a small herd of horses trotted around.

We set up camp by a creek and Meo and I bathed in the cold, clear water as the men prepared dinner. By 7.00pm it was dark and within a couple of hours we retired to bed. But it was another restless night as the surroundings were even noisier than in the village: cow-bells tinkled, crickets sang and frogs croaked.

'You are not cold?' came the greeting the next morning. It was pleasantly cool, like a British morning in June. As I rolled up the sleeves on my shirt, Meo looked askance. My girl guide instincts took over and I set to work dismantling the tents. 'Leave those', said Jak, 'they will do them'. He pointed to the porters sitting huddled around a fire, swathed in every bit of clothing they had, with woolly hats pulled down over their foreheads. I carried on.

After breakfast we set off, climbing a steep hill and then following a high ridge. We could hear monkeys whooping but could see little of the wildlife that must have been there. Paluepor talked about the environment and was very aware of the issues. He mentioned that about eighty per cent of the hilltribes now understand that they should not cut big trees. 'Taking the trees away leads to flash floods that ruin crops in the valleys', he explained, through Meo. 'And some of the creeks have dried up. I never used to believe what we were told, but now I have seen it with my own eyes.' We passed the occasional grove of trees, tied with

Taking The Trunk Road

saffron-coloured cloths and Meo explained, 'They have been ordained. The monks have blessed them and the people know not to cut or burn them'.

Paluepor talked of the wildlife that had roamed in the area. He pointed to a valley that had been the home of elephants, and we stopped at a high wooden platform which had been used as a tiger lookout by herdsmen guarding cattle. 'They've gone from here now . . . but there is still a tiger on that hill over there.'

By mid-afternoon we reached a village of Black Lahu people, perched on a dusty plateau. It had not had many visitors but had a spare hut in anticipation of any trekkers coming through. Meo and I settled in and then went to find the shower and toilet which, we were told, were at the other end of the village. A water tank had been installed on the next hill, and water was piped to a few points in the village.

After a thorough wash under the tap, I made my way back to our hut and was followed by several of the women from the village, along with their children. They sat around me in a semi-circle as I combed my hair and liberally applied moisturiser. I passed the tube around and each, in turn, rubbed the cream over their own arms and faces, and those of their children. Within minutes we all smelt like a branch of Body Shop and were smiling and giggling.

In the morning, returning from the 'bathroom', another woman stopped me. She turned my arm over and stroked my white skin, chatting away all the time. She then prodded me in various places on my body as if to check I was made of the same stuff as her. As Paluepor and Uncle washed the elephant at one of the village taps, a small crowd gathered to watch. Pat, meanwhile, had found a stick and grasping it in his trunk, was diligently cleaning his teeth.

It was not the best of days. I developed a headache and, as we brushed against trees, I was relentlessly covered in ants. We stopped for lunch but were attacked by a variety of biting bugs. It was a relief to set off again. I decided to walk but was soon slipping. Another stick was made and as we descended a long steep hill Uncle gently held the back

123

of my shirt, as if I was an errant child.

In the heat off the afternoon we reached a good spot to camp in a clearing set above a fast stream. Uncle cut some banana leaves and laid them on the ground as mats for myself and Meo. 'They are very cool', he explained. Sure enough they were, and we settled down for a short siesta. After washing in the stream and having an early dinner, there was little to do. Meo, whose father has gone back to being a monk, compared the experience to being a person of God. 'The simple life, the vegetarian food . . . and no alcohol.' At 7.00pm we went to bed. As I laid out my sleeping bag a hand passed me a loo roll and a bottle of water. Solicitous as ever.

Breakfast was like a scene from a cooking programme as rival teams prepared dishes over separate fires. On one a 'Western' breakfast was being prepared of cream of mushroom soup. Another fire was punctured with bamboo canes. Some were being used for boiling water for tea, others housed boiling eggs in the water, while a few were lined with banana leaves and were stuffed with steaming rice – regular long-grain in some, sticky rice in others. On yet another fire, a Karen-style curry was being prepared with the 'fruits of the forest' – wild ginger, banana shoots and a wild fruit that Meo had not seen before, had been added to some red onions, chilli, beans and tomato. A similar, yet subtly different curry was also being prepared – 'Lahu'-style. They were tasty but as Meo suggested, 'a bit strong for breakfast'.

After sampling every available breakfast, it was time to set off. We took a short trip through a deforested valley with an abandoned village, once the scene of a gun battle between opium-growers and the military, before hitting a broad track that led to our final village, home to some Lisu people. We arrived in time for lunch and after a siesta we went down the hillside to another larger Black Lahu village. This had a substantial vegetable field complete with 'greenhouses', a man-made lake and a duck farm. Photographs along the side of the schoolhouse proudly showed one of the Thai Royal Family visiting the village. The King has an initiative to persuade the hilltribes to cultivate vegetables

Taking The Trunk Road

and flowers instead of opium. We had seen no sign of opium growing – I was told that it continues but always over some other hill, in some distant valley, well away from roads.

We wandered through the village, stopping at its small store for a cold drink. This was a relatively modern village – the chief's house had a satellite dish, the occasional pick-up was driven through the village and there were plump horses and mules tethered around. An information centre had posters showing the effects of deforestation. Although we could hear the familiar thump of the manual rice mill, over at the far side of the village, there was a privately-owned mechanised one as well. As we walked back through the sandy streets Meo commented, 'we won't be able to make jokes about the hilltribes anymore'.

I awoke at 5.00am to the now familiar sounds of rice being milled and roosters crowing. It was still a couple of hours until sunrise but the village was already stirring. After breakfast a crowd gathered as the elephant was washed, and then a small *posse* followed us as we set off. I looked back to see a small boy holding up two tiny mewing kittens, as if to show them the elephant.

Breaking away from the well-worn track, the vegetation soon became denser and we slowly, and sometimes painfully, made our way through a tangle of thorn bushes and bamboo stands. At one point Pat resorted to pushing down a whole tree. After descending to a river we followed its course. Ghostly egrets took off at our approach. Kingfishers, each with their own territory, became more common as we entered woodland. Occasionally, just as we least expected to see people, we passed someone fishing – but not with a rod. Instead, wearing goggles, they would duck their head under water and grab the fish with their hands. A dog backed into the river with shock as we passed by and then barked until we were well out of sight.

We broke out into cultivated land and stopped for lunch on the riverbank. Pat found a short stick and with his trunk, gave himself a pedicure, cleaning out the dirt from between his toes. As I watched

Paluepor wash him, it dawned on me that this was where we were to say goodbye. A raftsman waited to take Meo and me back to 'civilisation'.

Paluepor ran to the edge of the bank as we pulled away and shouted something out. 'It's a blessing', explained Meo. Before I could respond we had drifted downstream. I knew that I was going to miss the elephant but nothing had prepared me for the tug I felt I leaving Paluepor, Uncle and the others behind.

Waking To Dreams Of Monglar

by Juliet Coombe

Rangoon, Burma's capital city, was a buzz of activity. The dingy hole-in-the-wall tea shops were decorated with red betel nut juice which had been splattered on the walls by old Burmese men, in between sips of coffee from saucers and cosy chats. Thirimingala Zei, the early morning market, was overflowing into the surrounding streets. Lotus flowers drowned in the decaying vegetables strewn over the ground, releasing a pungent smell. Woman dressed in shimmering silk *longyis* (tight sarongs) delicately picked their way through the crowds, pushing bicycles with live chickens attached to the handle bars and fruit balanced precariously in wire baskets. The Shwedagon Temple loomed, golden and glittering, in the background. At every major intersection, soldiers stood behind makeshift barbed wire barricades and kept an unflinching eye on passers-by, reminding me that the easy-going smiles of the market masked a deep fear.

As my taxi passed the Shwedagon Temple, I saw Buddhist devotees removing their shoes before making their way up the marble stairs leading to the summit of the pagoda. Pilgrims were buying tiny bamboo cages of birds to be released for good luck, and I tagged on a wish of my own as one flock circled and disappeared into the haze. On my way to the airport to fly to Kengtung, in the heart of the Golden Triangle, on the accident-prone Myanmar Airlines, I would need all the help I could get.

The airport was full of military officers that morning and a chaotic crowd was having to endure endless security checks. Frilly underwear and toiletries littered the counter as each overstuffed bag was opened and searched for contraband and material considered subversive by the government. My luggage was weighed on an ancient pair of scales and the immigration officer pointed out that my visa was close to running out. Muttering in inaudible Burmese, he eventually stamped my passport and waved me through bad-temperedly. The lounge area was full of orange, blue and red plastic chairs which seemed to have been designed to be as uncomfortable as possible. However, my discomfort was negated by the commanding view of the runway, where ground staff directed planes with pristine white gloves.

The lounge was crawling with soldiers, machine guns hanging from their shoulders and the occasional gold tooth glinting as grimaces masqueraded as smiles. A general stalked across the tarmac from a recently landed plane. Carrying a white cat, he looked remarkably like an ultra-sophisticated villain from a James Bond film. Everyone, even the elderly passengers waiting to board, sprung to their feet. He swept out of the building trailing his entourage, a bevy of suitcases and a military escort. The silence was broken only by the laughter of children, who looked incongruous in hand-embroidered bonnets, sporting the traditional, yellow *thanaka* facial paint as they waited for their flight.

The toilets in Burma are called 'rest rooms', which is ironic as they are often just holes in ground and there is nothing restful about squatting. After my seventh cup of sweet tea I had little alternative but to take my place in the queue. It was a further hour's delay before my plane finally arrived and, to my horror, the only safety checks appeared to be spinning the propeller and tapping the wings with a screwdriver.

Waking To Dreams Of Monglar

Luckily, nothing fell off, even when the maintenance engineer hit the fuel tank with a hammer and nonchalantly smoked a cheroot whilst filling it up.

The aircraft appeared to be a remnant from the days of the British Empire. It had armchair style seats and a thick black line labelled 'cut around this' circled the escape hatch. The tray-table had long since fallen off and the sign stating 'Your life vest is under your seat' was hopelessly optimistic. I looked out of the cracked windows and prayed this would not be my last view of Rangoon. Two Myanmar Airlines planes had already crashed that year due to poor maintenance and the British Embassy travel advice was to avoid using them.

The plane appeared to fly very low and I felt that any minute now we would collide nose-first into a hill. However, at always the very last moment, the plane would swoop up, narrowly missing a collision. Flying so close to the ground gave me a fantastic panoramic view of the patchwork paddy fields below and the stunning mountain ranges; the hide-away of the remote tribal people.

The air hostess walked along the aisle, restrained by her tight blue *longyi*, carrying tartan boxes with 'J'Donuts' enscribed on them. Give the Burmese a chance and they will copy anything. Even MacDonalds has been plagiarised into a Burmese fast food chain called 'Mac Burger'. Inside the box was a circular donut, a Lotte sweet and a chunk of cake called 'Butter Fresh'. To wash it down, the air hostesses provided cups of sickly-sweet Burmese tea.

The Burmese clapped as we landed on the well-worn potholed tarmac. The army came out to greet me. 'Passport, passport, checking, checking', they yelled. I dutifully handed it over for the usual range of paperwork. As I left the airport, I reached in my pocket for a scrappy piece of paper with the address of an English-speaking trekking guide named Harry, that had been given to me in Thailand. I approached the local taxi mob with trepidation, knowing full well that I was in for a few rounds of torturous haggling. Finally, I was driven in a beaten up Toyota to Harry's Adventure Trekking Guest House at 132 Mai Yang Road, Kanaburoy Village. It took ten minutes to get into the centre of town and a few more to Harry's simple but charming abode. I was thrilled to stay in such picturesque surroundings. It felt like home from home. Harry had coffee on tap, a kitchen to cook in, a water pump in the yard for washing and motorbikes to go out and explore the Golden Triangle.

I decided to make the most of the cooking facilities and knock up a stir-fry. Shopping at the local range of side stores was a far cry from a Western supermarket; one specialised in meat, another in vegetables and another in drinks. Sitting cross-legged, cutting up vegetables and listening to Harry talk about his many adventures and myriad of secret places across the mountains ranges, only made me more excited about exploring this remote part of Southeast Asia.

By 9.30pm everything was closed and most people asleep. In Kengtung everything starts as early as 3.00am, even the five-day-a-week market. The best, and perhaps only way, to see the area is by motorbike as due to the shocking state of the roads, it takes days to go anywhere by car or truck. In many cases transportation is impossible and one can only get to certain areas by foot, requiring many hours of trekking. At the end of the world it seemed like anything was possible with the only limitation being one's fear of the unknown – whether eating snake with the Lahu or trying Black Dog with the Akha hill tribe people.

The next morning I hired a bike and decided to go in search of the notorious town of Monglar and to discover some of the hilltribe communities along the way.

Monglar, a town on the Burmese-Chinese border, declared itself a 'democratic free zone' three years after Aung San Suu Kyi won the 1990 elections but was denied the right to govern by the military junta. Monglar, Burma's only 'liberated' town, was transformed in 1993 from two sleepy, innocent villages into one huge den of iniquity run by army generals, where drugs, gambling and prostitution have given it the nickname of Southeast Asia's Amsterdam. The fact that such a place could exist in Burma, which had such a strong traditional Buddhist culture and where the people were so noble, is baffling, and needs to be seen to be believed.

Burmese currency (kyat) is useless in Monglar, despite it being a

Waking To Dreams Of Monglar

Burmese town. Changing money into Chinese yuan before departing is essential in order to pay the army bribes along the way. It is ironically called a road tax but travelling along the rough mountainous paths one would have to be a fool not to realise that all the money goes towards the drugs and arms racket instead of road improvement. I felt a bit like a bandit myself, with dark glasses and a spotted handkerchief tied around my face to protect it from the dust.

I was only a few miles down the road when I heard music in the distance and decided to stop and explore further – after all, I had all the time in the world to get to the Chinese-Burmese border. Bang went the bamboo stick as the cymbols jangled together. Following the symphony of music, I discovered a group of Akha tribal women circling while moving their hands in all directions as their glittering ornamented head-dresses caught the early morning light, lending their mythological style helmets a glorious mystical glow.

I hid behind a fence, watching the men of the village smoking tobacco through bamboo pipes as they watched their women dance. The Akha maidens pounded their feet, spinning and whirling through the dust in synchronisation as they circled past me. Their colourfully embroidered tribal clothing enchanted all who watched the elaborate wedding ceremony.

One old woman spied my hidey-hole and approached me with a large glass of rice whisky. It looked lethal but I had little choice but to down it in one. The sweet liquid set my body on fire and inflamed my already sun-baked cheeks, turning them rosy red. In sign language she beckoned to me to join in so I walked around to the side of the property and a couple of children pulled open the bamboo fence. Before I knew it I was being dragged into the inner circle, twisting and turning to the beat of the drum. It had seemed so simple to an outsider's ignorant eyes but it was more complex than I had imagined, as every step seemed to hold a special meaning.

I felt trapped, unable to escape as all the women giggled and stared at me, passing over a bamboo stick for me to hold during the next dance. The oldest woman in the group showed me a series of intricate steps before the music started again. Inside the house the fifteen year old bride was being prepared to receive her marital headpiece. I noticed, as we danced on, that each head dress was slightly different. The chief ornaments were silver buttons, balls and old silver coins from India, French Indochina, Burma and Thailand. The amount of silver symbolises the wealth and social position of the man the Akha woman is to marry. Some are worth thousands of American dollars and are so heavy that it is surprising the women can lift their heads off the pillow, let alone dance like fairies. In addition, materials such as red gibbon fur, chickens, feathered tassels, colourful red and white beads, and seeds from the forest adorn these majestic head dresses. In the Akha community the man buys the head dress for his wife and from the day she puts it on it must stay on, even if she is in bed or working in the field in the height of summer. She can only remove it for cleaning or repairing, anything else is viewed as deeply shocking. However, even in the the most remote cut-off areas of Burma, these traditions are changing fast but one felt at this auspicious occasion that time had stood still and age-old customs were being upheld.

As I danced, the pace of the music became more frenetic as yet more glasses of rice wine were served. All around us the headman and elders had started snacking on rice, noodles and papaya salad, freshly prepared at the market. Sipping glasses of rice whisky out of old water, gin and rum bottles, they laughed and exchanged stories.

As the cymbols were passed to me I realised that I had met some of the women in the circle before. In fact, it was over breakfast at the morning market when I had been quietly chewing on some beef noodles and drinking sweet black coffee. Three Akha women had walked past carrying baskets full of sticky rice, cucumbers, spices, several kilos of noodles and bottles of well-fermented rice whisky. I remembered the incident clearly because instead of passing by, they accosted me. I thought, at first, that they were fascinated by my fair hair and skin but they were after my Vietnamese Hmong hilltribe silver necklace. Pulling at it like a chain and circling it in their well-worn hands, I felt like a prized bull. Their men watched patiently as they offered me 500 kyats

Waking To Dreams Of Monglar

(about US$1.50). I stood silently, not knowing what to do, as the bid rose from 1,000 to 3,500 kyats. As the price increased, so did the crowd, pushing and shoving to see what bauble had caught the women's eagle eyes. I relaxed and started to join in, gesturing jokingly for their headdress in exchange. The price continued climbing and just when they were running out of fingers, one woman took out a child's bonnet, beautifully hand embroidered, and offered it to me. As I turned it over in my hands, the early morning light caught the old Burmese coins, and the rotating movement caused the money and balls to collide. I do not know what stopped me; perhaps on reflection my soul told me it was not right to take the bonnet off them. As I passed it back they looked down in disappointment but then shook my hands in a way that suggested I had made the right decision. Perhaps they had wanted to buy it as a wedding present for their fifteen year old friend.

As the wind blew and the sun reached its highest point, I felt joyful that despite British colonisation, wars and oppressive military governments, the Akha community had managed to maintain and observe many of their customs. However I simultaneously wondered how they would cope with the modern world of technology and communication that increasingly encroaches on their world. As one headman succinctly put it, 'computers won't help my people plant the land or hunt for meat'. The hilltribe people have their own education system, passed down by the elders of the village.

Yet their ability to survive on the edge of the Golden Triangle shows an incredible inner strength that even the hardest Westerner would find impossible to match. Further, Kengtung, without its colourful hilltribe people would just be another ugly Asian town with no soul. If Burma, Thailand and Laos want tourism then they must realise that the Akha traditions are a vital attraction. For me, the memories of dancing in the Bang Yao village at the foot of the mountains was far more special than the ancient ruins of Pagan or Golden Shwedagon. For it is those proud and passionate people that make the Golden Triangle so magical and make my feet want to dance Akha-style.

Returning to the motorbike, slightly tipsy from the rice wine, it took a further forty-five minutes along the potholed Kengtung road to a bridge made from bamboo with woven slats. It swayed from side to side as I slowly made my way across, moaning under the weight of the bike. A couple of slats broke and fell into the fast moving water below. I was glad the old bridge still had enough strength in it to hold up whilst I dragged my 'Honda Dream' onto the opposite bank.

After resting for a couple of minutes, I started the long climb into the twisting mountain ranges that act as the perfect natural border between Burma and China. From here the roads deteriorated and the adrenalin rush of driving fast enough to miss the bumps, without skidding and being thrown over the edge, made the fifty-six mile bike ride an unforgettable journey.

In contrast to the Golden Triangle region around the Kengtung area, there were very few hilltribes in the mountains and I made only one more stop at Khara Village. On the surface it seemed similar in layout to so many other hilltribe communities in Kengtung. However, this village was hundreds of years old. In one of the three temples, there was a thousand year old rock where a group of pilgrims lit candles and chanted as they walked clockwise around the outer shrine. The golden rock was protected by sticks covered in peacock feathers, paper dragon symbols and dried flowers. The paintings on the wall looked like prehistoric drawings, delicately painted in gold and red. Their symbolic importance had long since been lost and as the monks opened the wooden doors, letting in shafts of light, I felt I was looking at Burma's equivalent of Australia's Ayers Rock. It sparkled as the streaks of sunlight caught the rim of the stone, creating a stunning dappling effect and I felt the animists spirits were awakening from their slumbers. As a monk hit the rock, one half echoed as the base remained solid and silent. It would take a geologist a lifetime to unravel the mysteries of this hilltribe village's sacred religious stone. For now I joined the pilgrims and lit a candle and prayed for a safe onward journey.

Back on the roads the dust flew from the big trucks, thundering along the broken tracks blasted out of the mountain granite. I felt sorry for the communities who still lived along this stretch of narrow, winding

Waking To Dreams Of Monglar

paths as the air was full of sand and dust clouds and I amused the border out-post guards no end, covered from head to toe with thick brown dirt. They found it hard to guess where I came from, and the guard looked genuinely surprised at my dishevelled state, especially when he discovered I was an English girl.

After the checkpoint there were many villages and hilltribe people to be found. They carried long knives for cutting crops and also guns. Even the women and children had rifles slung over their backs, whilst carrying babies in their papouches. The locals looked more facially Chinese after the border checkpoint, with oval faces and sleek black hair curled under simple scarfs. They wore field green skirts which provided the perfect camouflage in the sea of green paddy fields.

My body was bruised from the bumpy roads and I was glad after the seven-and-a-half hour ride to have reached Monglar before the sun had set. The town is a bizarre mixture of idyllic wooden hilltribe houses, with hole-in-the-ground toilets, no bathroom, a fire in the main room to cook on, and high-rise modern American-style, flashy concrete buildings, including luxury five-star marbled hotels. Turning into a back street, I found a family guest house. Being absolutely filthy, covered in yellow and red dust, I headed straight out to the river for a bath. The men in their red and blue underpants and the sarong-clad women looked serenely beautiful. But all was not as it seemed; the water was full of cattle waste, plastic bags and rubbish. It reminded me of bathing in the Ganges in India. The rich kids were washing their jeeps and Toyota cars in the water, further polluting it, while water buffaloes meandered through, stopping occasionally to take a drink.

Standing in the water, washing off the worst of the dust, I felt as if I was between two worlds. I was in a town on the edge of two very different countries, Burma and China, yet unlike either of them. It is a bizarre enclave that allows iniquities to pass untouched by the governing bodies of either country. A group of soldiers came down to the water's edge and I decided to take the opportunity to quietly slip away.

Back at the house, the family had prepared a simple meal and I was enchanted by the old man saying, 'if one person eats the food it does not

Intrepid Journeys

taste good but if many eat the meal it will taste delicious'. As the fire crackled I tucked into the coconut chicken curry, followed by a few rounds of rice whisky before braving Monglar by night. As I made my way down a dirt track and across a make-shift bridge, using the full moon as my torch, I found the glare of bright neon lights slightly unnerving. Out on the main tarmaced road was a mixture of open and closed shops selling expensive designer clothes.

Girls wearing short skirts or cut-off shorts with velcro or clingy trousers but always smothered in bright red lipstick, were chatting in doorways, rubbing the entrances with their long twig-like legs. Some women winked while others made sounds like cat cries. Their see-through tops revealed black sexy brassiere, making it only too clear to the business-men who passed them, that they were there for their pleasure. To my surprise most men hurried on, more interested in gambling than sex. After all, the hookers would be around at 5.00am, so what was the hurry? Ultimately money is money. I became aware of the watching eyes of soldiers checking out the proceedings from the rooftops, protecting us from goodness knows what. I felt like Monglar was indeed a seedier, more deadlier Amsterdam, where morality had taken a nose-dive.

The main street was full of colourful lights, a place where capitalism has turned two quiet villages into a bustling boom town. Sitting on a wall, I watched the pretty Chinese girls work the coffee shops and gambling tables. A 'session' here costs – particularly if she is a virgin – but in a town where everything is a gamble, no price is too high for the Chinese, Taiwanese, Thai and élite Burmese who flock here via the Chinese border. This is a place where drugs are described as medicine and gambling is a daily occupation. I asked the women what they felt about working in Monglar and one replied bluntly, 'the price for democracy is our souls, freedom is not free'. She then laughed nervously before adding, 'well not for us girls'.

Many of the prostitutes, some as young as eight, have been snatched from remote Chinese villages and forced into the racket. The girls do not get the money until they have been on the game for years, with most of

Waking To Dreams Of Monglar

it passing directly to the town's war lord generals. Sick of watching the hookers pawing and stroking fat old men with huge beer bellies, I headed for the main gambling tables to try my luck and see what the fuss was all about.

The dice was thrown again and again as key cards were called and yet more money was laid on the gambling tables, as more smartly dressed customers arrived until the place was heaving. Being the Year of the Tiger I placed a note on the relevant square and pulled on a rope. Out of the box three giant dice rolled and bounced into a plush red-carpeted area. Two tortoises and an elephant. My money was scooped away by the owner. Grinning, he called out 'any more bets?'. I abstained. Sadly, for many of the local people gambling had cost them a great deal more than a evening's entertainment. They were hooked, returning night after night to try their luck.

I wandered from table to table, listening to the banter and watching the wealthy Chinese, Taiwanese and Hong Kong tourists blow large amounts of money. Fortunes would change hands in a matter of seconds, while the players consumed plate-fulls of dumplings and steamed buns to sustain them for the next round. They would only leave the tables to enjoy some 'medicine', a polite way of saying they needed their nightly fix of the new designer drug, *yama*. High on drugs and adrenaline, a couple of plain-clothed guards hit on me and I made a quick escape down an alley.

Walking back to my family guest house, I realised how serious the effect of gambling, prostitution and drugs was on the local people, who found that the price of living had rocketed since the town had declared itself a 'Democratic-free zone'. This was the only place in Burma where my international mobile phone worked and where there were more soldiers than civilians. Yet, while in the rest of Burma freedom is a highly-prized goal, in Monglar the local people perceive freedom as dubious and corrupt.

Ten years ago the hilltribe people lived off rice but as the area continues to expand, finding fire wood and water is forcing the villagers to go further and further afield. Nothing had prepared them for these shocking changes and the mother of the family I was staying with commented, 'once all the rice dries up maybe my daughters will have to go into prostitution as well, and my sons into the Generals' army'.

As I headed out of town the next day I passed a group of soldiers, their guns glinting in the sun. They marched passed little stalls selling tiger and snake skins, shells and live Armadillos. I sat on my motorbike taking stock of the situation, watching locals flinch and move away as more and more soldiers marched up the hill, into an area cordoned-off by barbed wire. Not one of them turned to look at me although I knew that each had registered my presence. Unlike the locals I did not need to flinch and cower behind my bike. As I put on my helmet and sped off on my 'Honda Dream', I realised how lucky I was to have the ability to escape that place that describes itself, ironically, as democratic and therefore free. In Monglar, freedom is not free.

Where The Dragon Descends To The Sea

by Craig Dixon

My girlfriend has disappeared into the jungle on the back of a stranger's motorbike. I do not know where she is and I do not know where I am. And I think four men are trying to poison me with the juice from a jar of pickled pondslime.

Panic? That's still a few stages away. But I have reached paranoid and sweaty and I am closing fast on shrill.

In the space of a few hours we have managed to break basic travel rules one (do not pay the ferryman until he gets you to the other side); two (know which side you are on) and three (both of you stay on the same side). Together.

I am feeling dizzy. It is probably the moonshine. Maybe it is the waterpipe, although I cannot detect anything that does not taste like pungent tobacco. I am struggling to keep smiling and fast losing energy for trying to make myself understood. My hosts have momentarily stopped trying to address me and are talking quietly amongst themselves, glancing at me and laughing. I understand only 'vang' and 'khong' – yes and no. Their body language speaks more eloquently.

Where once they were cross-legged, leaning forward, smiling broadly and nodding, now they are drawn back, hugging their knees, eyeing my clothes, my Thai silver bracelet and my hair. That occupies them for some minutes. One of them says something and the others look at my head, my beard, my chest and arms, my thighs. One speaks and the others laugh. 'Vang!' It is not threatening but I am tense. There is a little girl outside the door. She is no more than five, bare except for faded undies. Beneath a long, gleaming fringe her big black eyes stare as she sucks constantly on her right fist. I smile. She ducks her fringe and swings her shoulders, breaking eye contact while all the time keeping that fist firmly in place. Then she looks back and, when I glance away, she advances a step closer to the door. I remember something and rummage in my pack. They are all looking now and when I produce a packet of Wrigley's spearmint, their eyes light up, like I have pulled a rabbit from a hat.

The fisherman on my right, who seems to own the hut, takes the pack from me, turning it over, running a thumbnail along the foil-covered ends of the gum. I take it back and shake out the sticks, offering them. I hold my arm out towards the little girl, who tosses her shoulders and retreats down a step. My host is peering closely at his stick, inhaling the mintiness, bending and straightening it, enjoying the pliability. He is reading the packet, lips moving silently. His face grows still. 'Wash-ing-ton', he says and looks up at the three other fishermen, then at me. He jabs a finger at the packet, 'Washington'. They all bump heads over the packet, unsmiling, and in seconds they are darkly muttering, 'Washington, Washington'.

We did not go looking for the war in Vietnam but it was there even before we landed. Descending at Ho Chi Min City's Tan Son Nhat airport, one sees first the military-style nissen huts, then the choppers and jetfighters rusting at the edge of the tarmac. I shake away images of figures in black pyjamas emerging from tunnels at the edge of the airfield, firing from the hip as shell bursts punch light into the dark Tet night. Forget that, I tell myself. This is not a movie. Within hours we are drinking beer at roadside tables downtown and the war is everywhere. Vietnam is the world's biggest exporter of scrap metal, mostly old war ordnance. And half of it seems to be in the hands of a dozen youngsters

Where The Dragon Descends To The Sea

who surround our table, offering Zippos, second-hand watches, engraved shell casings, amazingly detailed choppers made from Coke cans (even the rotor-blades turn) and, disturbingly, dogtags. Hundreds of dogtags. Names, ranks and serial numbers threaded on wire and held in bunches in the small, brown hands of children. I must look shocked. Lars, a friendly Swede, leans towards me and says: 'I read that most of this stuff is made in little places here in Saigon. They pay kids to jump on them, scratch them (he scruffs the sole of his boot on the ground) and then they put them in the rain to rust, so they are looking like the real thing'. I want to believe it.

We warm to Phuc and his family from the moment we storm into their guest house. They can barely conceal their delight when nine of us pile out of a taxi and clump through the door, all talking at once, pumping Phuc's hesitant hand and yelling introductions over each other's head. Then we all cram corridors and burst into rooms, following the entire family who watch intently for our reactions as they pat mattresses and turn water taps on and off. Mick and I fight off the others to claim the huge double room on the corner, overlooking an impossibly busy, roaring roundabout. We bargain well and graciously, as you do when you are happy and excited, and soon I am again clutching the embarrassed Phuc's hand to seal the deal. 400,000 dong for seven nights, up front (about US$6.00 a night). Bargain. We all agree to stay. Phuc's mother, Ba, claps her hands. I grab Phuc by the shoulder. 'Come with us for a beer, Phuc. How do you say beer in Vietnamese?'

'Bia.'

'Right-o then. What's the best bia?'

'The best?' Phuk smells a good deal 'Three three three', he smiles. 'We say "Ba Ba Ba".'

And we all dash out to find a Ba Ba Ba.

Several Ba Ba Bas later, Phuc's horrified. 'You are a spy?' he says, eyes widening.

'No, I write for a newspaper', I explain. 'I write, er, many things. Travel, crime, um, politics.'

His eyes widen again. 'Politics?' He is backing off, looking around. 'What for? Police? Soldiers?'

Christ. I imagine one of the kids hawking war trash around our table quietly slipping off and returning with a Communist Party apparatchik keen to nab a foreign enemy of the people.

'Phuc, I am not here to write about Vietnam. I am on holiday.'

Blank. 'Vacation?'

'Yes. In my country, working for a newspaper is not the same as working for the government. The government does not own the newspaper.' He looks doubtful but leans forward again in his seat, peering past a clutch of dogtags held between us by a six-year-old.

'You not write about Vietnam? Maybe you write about me?'

Phuc's got contacts in the Party. Ba, his mother, is a hero of the reunification struggle. The guest house is a gift to her from the government in gratitude for her efforts during the American war when, as a corporal in the South Vietnamese army, she spied for the Viet Cong. And that is not the least of it. While she maintained her dangerous double life, her husband was underground on the Ho Chi Minh Trail. Communication with him was impossible but she was excited one day when a fishseller who came to her door, passed on a message. Her husband wanted to meet her in a downturn Pho shop. She went and waited. He did not come. She never heard from him again. It is certain, she says quietly, that her husband was buried somewhere in the jungle along the Trail, along with thousands, hundreds of thousands, of other fighters who will never be found. And this, she smiles, spreading her hands to indicate the guest house, is her reward. The right to engage in capitalism, to make money from foreigners.

In Hanoi, we heard that gangs of youths sometimes harrassed travellers, especially late at night. We never experienced this. But, from the moment we arrive in Haiphong, we are on the defensive. The people we meet in Haiphong reflect their city – quiet, hardened, worn. It feels small and even though the city proper is not large, Greater Haiphong, which is the industrial centre of the north, makes Haiphong the country's third largest city. Fish and cement are the big businesses here. And we get the feeling tourism will soon rank right up there with the major export dollar earners.

The value of Haiphong's port was recognised early by Vietnam's enemies and as a consequence, Haiphong has a lot of experience with foreigners – the type of foreigners who send bombs and shells. The

Where The Dragon Descends To The Sea

French started the trend in 1946, just a year after reaching an agreement with the Viet Minh leader, Ho Chi Minh, to resume control of the country after Japanese occupation. One day, French aircraft appeared over the town and bombed civilian areas, killing about 600 people. It was an atrocity that led directly to the eight-year Franco-Viet Minh war. From 1965 to 1972, US Strategic Air Command sent bombers almost nightly over Haiphong. The American Navy lay thousands of mines in the fishing grounds. And it was in Haiphong that North Vietnamese volunteers would attend their own funerals before climbing into small outboard motorboats and setting out to ram mines. Watching the rice paddies pass on the three-hour train trip from Hanoi, I see a worker resting in the shade beneath the tail of a crashed B-52. The symbolism's almost too rich.

Our guest house turns out to be a medium-sized hotel. There is a big Communist Party regional gathering in town and the ground floor restaurant has been turned into a conference centre. Every hotel in Haiphong is full, the man behind the counter tells us. Here, there is only one room left. Surprise, surprise, it is the most expensive. At US$35.00 a night, it is the highest price we will pay in Vietnam for a night. But it has a TV and a bathroom and breakfast is served in our room. Mick is hooked. We are planning to catch the ferry to Bai Chay tomorrow, so one night of luxury will not hurt. We sign in.

Showered, fresh and hungry, we go downstairs to eat. The tables are in rows, covered with white paper and decorated with glass bowls and frangipani flowers. Two men in suits are eating at one end. Stoney-faced, they watch us enter. We smile and nod. No reaction. We sit at the end of a row and wait. After a few minutes, a woman appears with two steaming bowls which she puts before the two men. She disappears again without looking at us. Five minutes pass. No waitress. The two men speak quietly between mouthfuls, chopsticks clicking. On the wall above Mick is one of those classic kitsch seventies paintings – wild stallions galloping across a prairie beneath storm clouds. The horses have Asian eyes. Mick is starving. She goes to the door and calls. The waitress dawdles out. 'Can we have a menu please?' Mick asks. The woman looks blank. 'We want to eat', says Mick, miming. No reaction. The woman turns and disappears. 'And two Cokes', Mick says to her retreating back.

Intrepid Journeys

We wait another five minutes before the manager appears.

'Yes?'

'Two Cokes and two menus please.'

'No menus.'

'Okay, what can we eat?'

'Kitchen closed.'

'Closed?' I say and look pointedly at the two diners at the other end of the room. 'It's open for them.'

'No cooking. You have sandwich.'

'Yes, a chicken, cheese and tomato sandwich', says Mick before my impatience erupts. 'And a Coke.'

'No chicken.'

'What is there?'

'Egg.' Mick is allergic to eggs. Now she is getting edgy.

'Only eggs? I want what they are having.' She nods towards the men.

'I bring tea. Yes?'

Mick looks at me. I look at the Vietnamese horses. 'Yes, tea. And two Cokes.' We take them to our room.

An hour later we come down to find the conference room full. Waiters bustle around with big trays of fried prawns, steamed fish, fresh, crisp vegetables and enormous bowls of rice. Mick has got murder in her eyes but the manager is nowhere to be seen. 'Here we go', she says and heads straight into a gap in the crowd, moving determinedly down the rows of astonished communists and grabbing a vacant chair. In two seconds she has a mouthful of prawns. 'Mmm, excellent!' she says, as I squeeze in next to her. A well-dressed woman opposite stares at Mick as if she is the ghost of Ho Chi Minh. 'Chao Anh', Mick says to her and shoves in another crustacean. A waiter brushes past with a tray of enormous orange crab claws. Mick lifts it from his hands.

To their credit, nobody asks us to leave. I think they enjoy watching us enjoy the food so much. But when the speeches are about to start, we rise, bow and leave. Outside, the breeze carries a stench of fish and diesel from the harbour. The streets are crowded and the shops brightly lit. Within seconds, children fall in behind us. This is nothing unusual. In Saigon, at the zoo, we walked around staring at the monkeys and the hippos, while the other humans stared at us. You get used to it. But this feels different. There are teenagers among the group following us. Once, twice, someone steps on the back of my thongs, making me stumble. Laughter follows. I turn, smiling but looking hard at the older boys. We keep walking. I glance at Mick. She looks back, trying to smile but I sense her fright. As we reach a corner, we are stopped by a stream of people coming the other way. Mick steps out on to the road. Two men on a bicycle appear out of the traffic and, as they pass, the pillion passenger raises an open hand, swinging at Mick's face but missing as she flinches. In seconds, the older boys surround us. Behind them, I see adults watching. 'Horseface!' a voice shouts and the kids start chanting, 'Horseface, horseface'. A woman steps forward, pushing a little girl in a party dress. Shyly she looks up her mother, who whispers in her ear. Then, boldly, she runs up and grabs Mick's blouse. 'Give one dollar!' Mick takes the girl's hand. 'No dollar', she says angrily. 'You', she points at the woman 'Why do you make your child beg?' but her voice is lost as they all take up the cry. 'One dollar, one dollar, one dollar.' I look at the taunting face of the nearest older boy. Grabbing Mick's arm I step up until my face is centimetres from his. His gaze wavers and I press forward, forcing him aside. We slip out of the circle and walk steadily away. The 'one dollar, one dollar' chant follows us for a block but then the mob loses interest and within ten minutes we are back in our room.

Next day, we take the six-hour boat trip to Bai Chay, a lovely cliffside town on the edge of Halong Bay. On board, we strike up a conversation with a French student who recommends a trip out to Cat Ba, the largest of Ha Long Bay's 3,000 islands where there are empty beaches, caves, waterfalls and a huge national park teeming with birds and monkeys.

Within an hour of landing, we have negotiated with a fisherman to take us to Cat Ba town, six hours from Bai Chay. Next morning, we meet our skipper, who wants US$20.00 for diesel. We pay and settle on the deck for the journey. The sun is warm but a fresh northerly knocks the tops off a low swell. We get down out of the wind and are soon asleep. Mick wakes me as the boat's engine changes down a note. Dazed we looked around. We are chugging into a river mouth, the water clear and shallow. On the bow stands the deckhand, plunging a long bamboo pole into the clear water, gauging its depth. Tangled jungle comes down to the water's edge on both sides. There are no signs of civilisation. 'That didn't seem like six hours', says Mick. I look at the skipper. 'Cat Ba?' 'Cat Ba.' He does not meet my eye but swings the wheel and puts the engine in neutral.

We had read Cat Ba town was a big fishing village, with mini-hotels and guesthouses, bars and restaurants. Perhaps it is well back from the shore, hidden by the jungle. Mick is not fooled. 'This can't be it. Where are the hotels and bars and . . .' 'Maybe we're just stopping to pick someone up', I say, not even convincing myself. The deckhand goes to the stern, draws in the rowboat tender and lowers in our packs. 'Hey', says Mick. 'We want Cat Ba Town.' 'Cat Ba', says the skipper and points to the shore. We look and see a narrow gravel track come out of the jungle and down to a small, timber boat ramp. The deckie's in the tender, beckoning us to climb in. 'What do you reckon?' I ask Mick. 'There's something shonky going on.' 'Yeah. Should we stay on board?' We look at each other. The deckhand's saying, 'yes, Cat Ba. Come'. 'We'll go ashore. You stay in the rowboat and I'll have a look. If there's nothing there, we'll come back.'

On the beach, Mick scrambles up the path and disappears for a minute or so. She comes back with news that there is what appears to be a small store with a motorbike parked outside. As soon as we lift out our packs, the deckhand pushes off, waving and smiling and pointing up the track, 'Cat Ba. Cat Ba'. The shack is locked. We call out but there is no answer. It is incredibly hot. No wind stirs the palm tops and the air vibrates with insect calls. We walk further along the track and suddenly an ancient woman appears, her back bent and her face incredibly lined. But her eyes, deep in the shadow of a conical hat, smile brightly. 'Chao Anh.' We point up the track. 'Cat Ba?' She motions to us to follow and sets a pace that has us sweating like horses. Twenty minutes later we reach a clearing in the jungle. There is a small green shack raised off the ground on half-metre stumps, a well and a chicken coup. An enormous sow lays beneath the house, grunting as ten or so piglets pack in a scrum around her belly. We hear voices and see, at the side of the house, some boys kicking a shuttlecock over a torn fishing net and two little girls trying to hold a wriggling piglet. The old woman shouts something and the kids all turn and see us. There is a moment's shock and then suddenly they all start running towards us screaming, scattering

Where The Dragon Descends To The Sea

squealing pigs and chickens. Four men appear out of the house, playing cards in their hands, wide-eyed at seeing two foreigners in the front yard. 'Anyone speak English?' I say. They all stare. 'English', mutters one of the men, looking Mick up and down. 'Where is Cat Ba', I ask. 'Cat Ba', they say. 'Motorbike?' I say, holding two fists out and revving an imaginary throttle. 'Taxi? Cyclo?' 'Cyclo!' they laugh, looking around at the jungle and the narrow dirt goat track.

There is no transport, we learn. But one of the boys runs off into the jungle. Mick and I play charades with our hosts, wondering if we will have to spend the night here, until we hear a motorbike coming down the track. One motorbike. Its rider, a young man in sunglasses cannot take his eyes off Mick. But he speaks a little English. He will take us to Cat Ba Town for US$20.00. We need two motorbikes, we say, pointing to our packs. No other bikes are available. I remember there is another at the shack near the boat ramp. 'No good', he says. Maybe we should start walking? 'Don't be ridiculous', says Mick.

'I'm not letting you go off alone with this bloke. Anything could happen. What if he just drops you somewhere?'

'Look, it'll be fine. We don't have much choice.'

'How far is Cat Ba Town?' I ask the biker. 'One hour? Two hours?' 'Yes.'

So Mick climbs on behind the driver, who spends an inordinate time putting on his sunnies and revving the bike, letting us all know how important he is and then they disappear into the jungle, leaving me tense and worried and imagining all sorts of terrible things.

He has been gone four hours. I leave the fishermen gazing at the world map I dug from my pack. I have made it very clear I am not American, pointing out Washington and shaking my head, drawing a line between Melbourne and Hanoi. Outside, even the chickens are weighed down by the heat. I draw a bucket from the well and rinse my head. It is late afternoon. In the sunlit treetops, a monkey screeches. Then I become aware of another noise. A motorbike! He's back! Immediately, my paranoia eases. I have not been poisoned, robbed and buried under the chicken shed.

I have never been so happy to see a place as I have Cat Ba town. Roaring down a steep hill and through the town gates, I see Mick outside a guesthouse. Relief floods over me. We pay the biker who heads for the nearest bar. I am exhausted and barely make the climb to our top floor room. The view is magnificent. The sun is setting and the molten sea rolls like mercury beneath the fishing boats. From the street drift cooking smells, music and the din of motors. It is wonderful but all I want is bed, which is lucky because, at that point, the electricity goes off.

Ha Long Bay is a place of legends. The locals believe a dragon swept down from the mountains and across the Red River Delta, its great tail carving swathes in the earth. As it plunged into what is now called the Gulf of Tonkin, the sea fell back, leaving only high ground uncovered. These high points are the 3,000 limestone outcrops that rise like pillars from the cool emerald waters. Another legend is of a beast called the Tarasque. Fishermen hand down stories of a mighty but benevolent creature that appears suddenly, its huge serpentine form breaking the waters and then disappearing. It is good luck, the fishermen say, to see the Tarasque. It guarantees a lifetime of full nets and wealth.

Ha Long Bay sparkles. We spend the day cruising from island to island, stopping to climb into magnificent, stalactite-hung caves, finding empty beaches, bartering with children in motorboats laden with blue crabs, dragon prawns, clams and mother-of-pearl.

Heading back to Cat Ba, passing junks with sails alight in the setting sun, we sit on the roof of the cabin and drink bia. Tomorrow we head back to Hanoi and a flight out of Vietnam. 'Bia Bia Bia!' I shout to the skipper as he cuts the engine. 'Vang!' he yells and we stride down the dock to the fishermen's bar. We drink beer poured over chunks of ice and share our cigarettes. There is a pool table on the cracked footpath, a single bare lightbulb strung above it. Mick wants to play and our skipper, foolishly, takes her on. Within minutes, half the male population has heard about the party and rushes down to join in. It must be the first time in their lives they have seen a woman not only drink beer and play pool, but beat all the contestants. 'When you go home', the fisherman tells me: 'Tell your friends: "Ha Long Bay number one, Cat Ba number one".' We clink glasses. 'Ha Long number one!' I cry, and the fishermen cheer as Mick pots another one.

A Romantic Landslide In China

by Ian Jackson

'Don't do it man, stay here for a week or two until everything is fixed. Don't go, it nearly killed us.' The Dutchman looked exhausted, in fact he looked completely knackered. His eyes were bloodshot and his hands trembled as he reached for a beer. He was caked in mud and his hands and legs were covered in deep cuts. Blood still trickled down his leg from a cut on his knee. His mate just nodded in agreement.

I wondered what had happened to him. The train from Hekou through the Vietnamese/Chinese border to Kunming was not that bad. Sure the cattle class that is hard seat travel on Chinese trains could be bad but he looked like he had gone several rounds with a group of Chinese grannies over a seat and lost – badly. I looked at the girls and wondered whether they were up to the rigours ahead.

About a week ago I had been sitting in a bar in Bangkok, now I was trapped in a remote Chinese town. I could not go back because it was a border town and I had no visa. I could not go forward because a massive landslide had cut off all roads and train lines. Fate can be a fickle friend.

Intrepid Journeys

I was flying to Hanoi to meet Hally, an old friend from home with whom I was going to be travelling to China. I was looking forward to seeing her, Hanoi and China again. Who would have changed the most since the last time I had seen them? Hanoi and the surrounding countryside looked different from the air, very different to how it looked the last time. It was green and verdant and the city sprawl seemed bigger than I remembered. The year before fate had put me on a motorbike. What would she have in store for me this time?

After a stroll around Hanoi I was desperate for sleep. I went upstairs to the dorm I was staying in and felt strangely alone but nevertheless drifted quickly into a deep sleep.

It felt like morning but I was not sure, nor was I game to opening my eyes. I was enjoying that half-asleep-half-awake feeling, the nether world between being aware and not being aware. I could hear voices, female voices. I listened but could not really make out what was being said. I rolled over and partly opened one eye. I opened both eyes. There she was, wearing a white 'Tin Tin in Vietnam' T-shirt, brushing her long, wet, dark hair. There were other people in the room but my eyes were drawn to the brush, the long hair and the smile. It was the smile of an angel. 'Hi, we were wondering when you'd wake up.' I sat up, rubbed my face and moved the China guidebook I had been trying to read the night before. 'Are you going to China? I'm going to China. Have you been? Do you know what the border's like? Where are the best places to go?' The questions were like rapid fire. I was still half asleep and could not take my eyes off that face. I was aware of other people moving around but I did not take them in.

'Yeah, I've been to China and I'm heading back. The border isn't a problem.' We chatted about China, Vietnam and travelling for what seemed like ages. The more we spoke the more I was intrigued. Something about her made me want the conversation to carry on forever but before I knew it she was gone, whisked away from me by her friends.

Over the next few days I saw her around Hanoi, we even talked briefly, always exchanging a hello and a smile but fate decreed we were always travelling around town in opposite directions.

A Romantic Landslide In China

Hally and I had to buy our visas from the Chinese Embassy. It was a austere, grey, concrete block. Stern-faced uniformed officials gave us forms to fill in. After answering dozens of questions we reached the counter.

'You can't go to Beijing.'

'Why not?'

'Too many people.'

Strange, you would not normally think the capital city in a country of God-knows-how-many-million would be crowded.

'You must get letter from China Tourist.'

'OK. Where are they?'

'China.'

'But if we can't go to China how can we get the letter from China Tourist?'

'You must have letter.'

Great, Chinese bureaucracy and we were not even there yet.

'OK, we won't go to Beijing.'

'You can have visa by next Wednesday.'

'But they are getting their visas on Friday', I said, pointing to the people in the next queue.

'No, Wednesday.'

'Will US$10.00 get us the visas by Friday?'

'You can get visas on Friday.'

Walking through the streets of Hekou I felt like a million dollars. The sun was shining and it was great to be back in China. I felt that I had been going soft after a few weeks relaxing on the islands in Thailand. I was looking forward to hitting the road, battling to achieve everyday chores. I was also looking forward to travelling through Yunnan province and up through the mountains of Sichuan and Gansu.

Hally was not with me but I was not unduly worried about finding her. I turned the corner of the main street and there she was. I should have known it would not be difficult. She was sitting at a street café drinking beer in the sun. She was with a group of other girls, all laughing, and a guy who sat quietly in the corner. She was with Tin Tin girl. My heart skipped a beat. We hugged each other. Finally, we introduced ourselves and then we all talked about the landslide, ate, drank and talked more about the landslide. There was only one real option open to us – to walk.

The rain lashed against the window. I looked at the others who were still asleep. It did not sound like a great day to be hiking seventeen kilometres through a landslide. Somehow, either through bad luck or stupidity, I found myself carrying the heaviest backpack while someone else got my half-empty one. 'Thanks', said Tin Tin girl. 'This is really light compared to mine.' 'Yeah, don't mention it. What the hell is in this thing?' She just smiled and headed off down the street laughing. I loved that laugh. We set off, full of enthusiasm for the long march ahead. It would not be that bad, would it? The Dutchman must have been exaggerating. We left town and hit a crossroads where we saw a group of Chinese men sitting by the road. They must have known something we did not so we stopped and sat down near them. They looked oddly at us for a few minutes and went back to their conversation.

Before long a truck pulled up which we all piled into. Landslide, ha. Maybe it was all a cruel hoax to get silly Westerners traipsing through the countryside. Why would a truck be heading that way if it could not get through? It became painfully obvious that we were deluding ourselves. Bouncing over the potholes, water splashing everywhere, we rounded a corner. Up ahead was our first sight of the landslide. Mud, large boulders and trees covered the road. We made our first tentative steps through the mud and sank ankle deep. The backpack was already weighing me down and I was covered in sweat. The jokes lessened and then stopped. I tried to keep the girls upbeat but it was a struggle. How much further to go? A Chinese man had been watching us and finally plucked up the courage to talk to me. His English was good and he said he would get us to the other side if we followed him. He was our guardian angel.

Finally we reached a sealed road. It was great to be out of the mud and enjoying the scenery. The countryside was beautiful and the sun was poking its head out from behind the clouds. On the side of the road was

A Romantic Landslide In China

a wooden shack-cum-noodle shop. Two guys were sitting outside playing cards and drinking Chinese tea. 'You wait here', said Guardian Angel. He jogged over and an animated conversation took place, fingers pointing in our direction. Guardian Angel walked back over. 'They carry bags for the girls', he proudly announced. 'You strong. You carry own bag.' Great. I save face by carrying a heavy bag and because I am not a girl I end up a crippled hunchback by the end of the hike. I do not care about this face-saving business, I want to be able to walk in later years. 'Thanks', I said through gritted teeth.

The card sharks put on a pack each, strapped two packs to a bamboo pole, hoisted the pole onto their shoulders and set off down the road. The girls, free from the weight of the backpacks attacked the hike with renewed vigour and enthusiasm. I just shook my head and walked off as Guardian Angel put his arm around my shoulder and talked about how good his English was.

Suddenly a massive drop lay in our path; the road had been completely washed way. We stood on the edge and stared down. Jesus, it was a long way down. We had been walking for about three hours and there was no way we were turning back and going through all that mud again, not when there was the chance that the road had not been destroyed on the other side of the canyon before us.

There was a small trail about the width of a pair of feet which followed the side of a steep cliff, narrowing as it reached the top before widening along the descent. One false slip would have had us careering over the side. Some people were coming the other way and warned us to hold onto whatever we could at the top. Two of the girls went first with Guardian Angel leading the way. I followed with Tin Tin girl and Hally, showing them where to step and what to hold on to. At the top we came across a French girl who was climbing towards us. 'How far is it to Hekou?' she asked. I was stunned. 'Aaargh, two or three hours, it isn't that bad.' 'Good. Did you see two French guys there? I'm supposed to be meeting them.' I was flabbergasted. This was not the place for idle chit chat. 'No, get out of my bloody way before I fall off.' I turned my back to the cliff and held on with both hands so she could get around

Intrepid Journeys

me. She was not carrying anything and made it around easily enough. 'What's the border crossing like, is it difficult?' 'Easy', I replied and made my way down before she could start asking any other dumb questions or before I pushed her off the cliff. I could not believe how stupid she was. What did she expect? The A-to-Z of crossing the Chinese/Vietnamese border while I balanced precariously on a muddy path, hanging onto tree roots to stop myself plummeting several hundred feet to my death?

Things were easier for the next hour or two as we walked along a road. It was tiring carrying the backpack and the girls were flagging. So was I. At least we were walking along a tar road and not dragging ourselves through mud. We were filthy and sweating in the afternoon sun. The thought that we were not far from transport kept us going and, rather like being marooned on a desert island, we talked about hot showers and what meals we were looking forward to. Our steps were getting smaller and the pace was slowing. The card sharks were still bouncing along in the distance and would stop every so often for a cigarette so we could catch up. They made it seem like they did this every other day. And to think I had been afraid of going soft and had wanted some hard travelling again.

Every time we turned a corner I hoped it would be the last one but Mother Nature was determined to test us once more. Another large section of the road had been washed out. Guardian Angel pointed to a trail that led up through the mountains. 'We go there. Not far to go.' We asked how far. 'Oh, maybe two hours. Not much. You OK?' 'Oh yeah, I'm fine. Big muscles, this pack is really light', and smiled the biggest false smile I have ever smiled. My body was aching. My shoulders felt like they were about to drop off and my legs were screaming at me to stop and sit down. I knew that would have been the worst thing I could have done as I would never have been able to get up again. I stumbled around with a cigarette, talking to Guardian Angel while everyone else lay on the road catching their breath.

We followed the trail up through the mountains, pushing branches out of our faces whilst trying to use them to steady ourselves. The path

A Romantic Landslide In China

followed the railway line – or what was left of it. Once again we were shin deep in mud, rocks and branches. Up ahead we could hear the muffled roar of explosions. Guardian Angel explained that the army was using dynamite in an attempt to blast their way through the landslide but reassured us that they would stop when we got closer. 'Well, that's a bonus', I thought. 'There has already been a landslide, people are walking through it and dynamite is exploding round our ears. Chinese logic can be a wonderful thing at times.'

Suddenly the end was in sight, or at least hearing. We all heard the trucks. Eureka! The end is nigh! Everyone perked up for the last couple of hundred metres. The abuse of all things Chinese stopped. A feeble joke or two was made. People smiled for the first time in hours. The finishing line was in sight. A last scrabble up a steep, slippery hill and we were there – the road and civilisation. Exhausted and elated everyone slumped to the ground. The thought of a papal kiss on the tarmac crossed my mind. We were covered from head to toe in mud, cuts and sweat but we did not care. We had made it. No one had any idea where we were but at least there was no more mud to walk through, no more cliffs to scale, no more silly French women to contend with and no more dynamite blasts to dodge.

As we were wondering how far it was to the first town and food, Guardian Angel hailed a passing tractor. We all climbed into a wagon at the back and relaxed. We were too weary to worry about where it was going. Tin Tin girl and I talked and talked. It felt like we were the only ones there.

We rode into Nanxi, a one horse town. Guardian Angel wanted to eat. We wanted to wash. We compromised. Two of us went into a restaurant with him while the others leapt into a fountain. Guardian Angel spoke rapidly to the owner and the plates of food started streaming out of the kitchen. I wondered who was going to pay for it all but was too tired and hungry to care. We ate and were happy.

Nanxi was a strange town. Guardian Angel visited three different hotels in an attempt to find us somewhere to stay. The first two were cold and grey and we had to wait for ages before they eventually told us we could not stay - Guardian Angel explained the owners would get in trouble with the police if they were found to be housing Westerners. He finally found us a small place on the other side of town. The showers were in a shed with four hoses hanging from the wall. The water was cold but no one cared. Refreshed, relaxed, hungry again and ready for a night on the town, we found a small restaurant to eat in and were quickly surrounded by an ever-increasing number of spectators. We put on a tape and started dancing with the women running the restaurant. Word got around and suddenly it seemed like half the town was watching us. It was great to be alive.

The next day we got a bus from Nanxi to Kaiguan. It took about eight hours but the winding mountain road provided stunning views of ravines, gorges and waterfalls. It was heavenly to have a numb bum, rather than sore feet by the end of the day. Furthermore, five people who had been virtual strangers a few days before were now great mates, laughing, telling jokes and sharing a lifetime of secrets with each other. We had a special bond. For some reason Tin Tin girl and I were even closer. There were shared looks, conspiratorial smiles and discussions about dreams. We talked, we laughed, we joked, we poked fun at each other. We became close, very close.

Two days later we were in Kunming. Suddenly one adventure was over and another was about to begin. Soon five became three, then two. Two who went on through China, Hong Kong, parts of Thailand, Malaysia, Indonesia, Australia and on to London. Along the way I was on bended knee asking Tin Tin girl to marry me. She said yes. Who said being trapped by a landslide was a bad thing?

Climbing Out Of The Jungle

by Steve Davey

I repeated the travellers' *clichés* in my mind over and over again. 'Suffering is character building'; 'Today's discomfort is tomorrow's dinner table anecdote' and even, 'It will all be over in the morning'. In truth, they did not help a bit. I was tired, soaking wet, covered in mosquito bites and I had just found an engorged leech feeding off my calf just below the level of my boot. This, at least, was something positive. It meant that I had a good excuse to ponce a cigarette from George, my guide, in order to burn it off. I had given up smoking a while before but was dying for a cigarette. George chain-smoked and after walking behind him all day, I had developed a real craving for his rough, local tobacco. Even this did not help. I was thoroughly miserable, and still had another three days to go until we reached Sandakan.

I had wanted to visit Borneo ever since an elderly relative had given me a couple of Dyak fertility shields. Carved out of a solid block of wood and adorned with human hair, they were an evocative image in my childhood. She had picked them up in Borneo when her husband was the

Intrepid Journeys

captain of a steamship in the South China Sea at the turn of the century. I wanted to travel to this strange and still partly unexplored land to see where these shields had originated.

Now I was not so sure. I was heartily sick of the jungle. For the past few days I had been struggling through the undergrowth, with a heavy pack cutting into my shoulders. This was no walk in the park. The track we were following, for as much as it existed, was often blocked by fallen trees and thick, thorny undergrowth. Not being the most co-ordinated person in the world at the best of times, I was covered in cuts, bruises and large red welts from a myriad of stumbles and falls.

At times we had to wade across waist-deep rivers and although I knew the dreaded pipe-fish lived in South America, I was still paranoid about picking up an unwanted hitchhiker. I could not remember the last time I had been dry. If it was not sweat from the exertion, it was water from the constant rain dripping from the trees, which towered over us and blocked out much of the sunlight.

Every night I would collapse under a mosquito net, completely exhausted, listening to the cacophony of the jungle chorus screaming, howling, clicking and chirruping. This was jungle, real jungle, and I had had just about enough of it.

I wanted to be somewhere dry, where I could see the sun and where there were no leeches. When one of my fellow hikers suggested I should take a trip to Mount Kinabalu in Sabah (North Borneo) it seemed like a perfect idea. Apparently the sunrise from the top of the mountain was one of the most spectacular sights on the island. What I was not told was that Mount Kinabalu, at 4101 metres, was the highest peak between the Himalayas and New Guinea.

I guess in the back of my mind I had visions of myself scaling a totally unspoilt mountain, alone with the elements, a couple of porters carrying my pack and my camera bag, leaving me free to stroll to the summit, taking a few pictures on the way. A few strenuous hours, then a glorious sunrise. Oh how we do like to dream.

Over 22,000 people a year make the ascent up Mount Kinabalu, which meant that dividing by 365 and allowing for the seasons, I was not

Climbing Out Of The Jungle

going to get the solitude I craved. What I was going to get was an Australian couple who were travelling around the world for a year before heading back home to inherit a farm which seemed to consist of a few thousand acres of cat litter tray and a couple of ramshackle buildings. There was a Danish woman and a Swedish woman in their late thirties who were probably a couple as well. They had the best of everything – and it matched! Royal blue and pillar-box red Gore-Tex windcheaters and waterproof leggings, insulated water bottles, 48-part Swiss army knives and rucsacs that were perfectly ergonomically balanced. I hoped that I was not the only one to feel disreputably shabby. The last of the happy climbers was an over-earnest English woman who seemed to have a fixation about finding some cider to drink. She kept breaking into a nervous little laugh after everything she said – most of which consisted of primary school level environmentalism. These were to be my companions on the assault of the summit.

Our guide was Sapinggi, a local who had been climbing the mountain for so many years that his calf muscles were bigger than my thigh muscles. Apart from these gargantuan appendages, he was short and wiry, and had the sort of irrepressible grin which could easily be confused with mockery if you are tall, broad and exceptionally unfit.

I did not realise that I was unfit when I started this climb. Like many people who had just strolled past thirty, I was convinced I was at the peak of physical fitness. Every organ in, and hanging off my body, honed to perfection. This damn climb certainly changed my opinion.

It all started to go horribly wrong at the briefing before we set off. On the first day we were going to walk up to the overnight hut at Laban Rata, ready for the final stroll to the top for . . . hang on, what was this, for sunrise? It all began to sink in. I had to walk for a whole day – upwards. Then I had to sleep in a cold hut, get up before dawn to walk for another two hours just to see the sunrise. I cursed my luck. I cursed my fellow hiker in the jungle who had dumped me in all this. Most of all I cursed myself. Instead of the welcome break which I had deserved for supporting the entire Borneo leech population on my nether regions for a week and despite a lingering case of what can only be described as trench foot, I had unwittingly accepted a challenge to hump a twenty-kilogramme camera bag up a mountain, just so I could photograph a sunset. I made a mental note to ask Sapinggi for a receipt. If I was going to do it then I was bloody-well going to tax deduct it!

The first Westerner to climb Mount Kinabalu was Sir Hugh Low in 1851. In a supreme irony probably lost on the locals, the highest peak was named after him. Whether any locals had climbed the peak before him has not been recorded but I suspect they had more sense. Things have changed somewhat since Sir Hugh's day. Now a rough path of stones and high steps lead up the mountain side. There are apparently 2,500 steps in all, although I lost count after about twelve. Memo to Nikon: can you please make the F4 lighter?

Just to make Westerners feel even more unfit and soft, someone has built freshwater stops and even shelters en route. I waited at one for about twenty minutes in the hope that a bus might come along but was finally driven out by Sapinggi and his evil grin.

To make matters worse, the locals fair ran up the mountain. Even the porters who were carrying supplies to the guesthouse at Laban Rata were outpacing our little party. Heavily-laden bamboo baskets hanging from their heads by a strap, they were bent almost double to support the weight. Their eyes were permanently focussed on the track in front, and if they wanted to look at us they had to raise their eyes to such a point that their foreheads creased in mock surprise.

On the way down the hill after delivering their loads, the porters took the steps at such a pace that they almost appeared to be floating. The upper halves of their bodies would glide by serenely, but their little legs would be pumping like pistons as they skipped from step to step.

Such is the degree of ease which they can conquer Mount Kinabalu that a Climbathon is held every September, when anyone with nothing better to do can race up and down the mountainside. A recent winner was five months pregnant. She won US$2,500 and a flight to London.

As we climbed higher up the mountainside we entered a belt of misty fog which clung to the path and followed the legs of the climbers in front of me in little eddying swirls. If it was not for the fact that I was

Climbing Out Of The Jungle

beginning to heave for breath from the rarefied atmosphere, I might have been taken by the mysticism and surreality of this moment – disappearing into the clouds which had disguised the mountain peak all day.

The heat and humidity from the earlier part of the climb was now a distant memory, or at least would have been if it had not been for the sweat-drenched clothes sticking to my back. I need not have worried as I was soon soaked by a fine drizzly rain which drove into my face.

The climb seemed to become even steeper before levelling out at the guesthouse at Laban Rata. By now my body ached and I was ready to drop. Our porters had long since arrived and unhelpfully flashed me encouraging grins, as I flopped down in the corner and pulled off my boots for a blister inspection.

I barely had the time to change into some dry clothes before we were all sitting down in a circle for a meal of noodles with a sauce, which, thankfully, remained unidentified. The rain was belting down outside and there was precious little to do save play cards and dream of being on a hot beach somewhere.

Sapinggi lit a fire and began to tell us of some of the beliefs of his people, the Duson. Mount Kinabalu is sacred to the Duson and they believe that it is the home of their spirit ancestors. When a villager dies, he or she is cremated and then the family prepares food for the deceased's spirit-journey. They make rice balls and roll them round. If the ball stays in one piece then the spirit is not happy. If a few grains fall off then all is well. If the whole rice ball collapses then it is an omen to expect a disaster such as a landslide or a typhoon. I hoped that the Duson rice-rolling skills were up to scratch as it was going to be an early and hard climb tomorrow. Every year, in an attempt to appease the spirits, sacrifices of seven white chickens, seven eggs, betel nut, tobacco and lime are made on the mountainside.

Soon after this, one of my fellow climbers suggested a sing-song, and I decided that it was time for bed. I could take the cold, I could take the wet, on a good day I could even take the physical exhaustion and the blisters, but a few choruses of *Kum By Ahhh* or whatever they were planning was just too much for me!

Luckily I had negotiated the mountain-top plumbing and was tucked up in my uncomfortable bed long before they managed to agree on a song to which they all knew the words, and gave in to exhaustion before they could disturb me.

I woke with a start as someone shook my shoulder. Blinking to wakefulness I had an awful realisation of where I was. Halfway up a mountain, cold and damp, and now trying desperately to wake up. I glanced at my watch. 2.00am. I lingered for a few more seconds under the blanket and then forced myself to get up. I thought my bed was cold, but the room was worse. I hurriedly tugged on the few clothes which I had taken off the night before and went to find a cup of coffee.

Sapinggi was waiting there with his usual grin. Did he have any idea how much I was suffering? My legs ached, and my calves had seized up so much I could barely limp. When I sat down on the chair next to him, my back and shoulders felt so sore, I groaned in protest.

It is amazing the things that you will do just because some insomniac writes about them in a guide book and makes them 'popular'. This was probably the fourth or fifth sunrise which I had viewed from the top of a mountain and yet I was still here in the hope that this one might be a little different. I had photographs of sunrise from volcanoes in Bali and mountains in Africa but had yet to sell any of them. What, I mused, kept bringing me back to all these dawn starts and excruciating exertions. I certainly did not enjoy it. I generally was not up to it, but I still kept doing it.

At around 3.00am we were ready to set off. By this time I was getting impatient and was ready to go. There is only one thing worse than climbing a mountain in the middle of the night to see the sunrise, and that is climbing a mountain in the middle of the night and missing the sunrise.

It was pitch dark when we set off, but after a while my eyes grew more accustomed to the moonlight and I could make out the hulking spectre of Mount Kinabalu in front of me.

The path was still wet and slippery from the previous day's downpour and the quiet of the night was punctured by hissed curses as

Climbing Out Of The Jungle

yet another tourist fell over. Most things seem exaggerated in the dark and the boulders which loomed over us were no exception. The darkness and the tales of the spirits from the night before cast an eerie mood over our little party as we made slow progress to the summit.

The path grew steeper, and soon we reached a section which was slung with ropes. This made the navigation easier, but soon the muscles in my arms were screaming out as much as those in my legs as I pulled myself up over the steep rock faces. The ropes were still wet from the rain, and this, combined with the biting wind had soon driven all feeling from my fingers. I had visions of myself losing my grip and plunging into the inky blackness below, but soon realised that it probably was not as dangerous as I imagined.

The climb seemed an interminable mix of cold and wet and physical discomfort, but for some reason none of us thought to turn back. It might have been stubbornness, it might have been drive and determination but I have a sneaking suspicion that we were all too tired and cold to think of it.

After what seemed like an eternity I hauled myself over yet another boulder and was met by Sapinggi wearing his most broad grin yet. 'Welcome to the top of Borneo, you have made it.' He was partly obscuring a small sign which marked the summit of the mountain. I should have felt a glow of pride but I had a nagging thought in the back of my head – if there was still forty minutes to sunrise, why the hell did I have to get out of bed so early?

As the stragglers arrived, we all sat huddled around the sign waiting for the sunrise. Thankfully no one suggested singing. The old *cliché* goes that the darkest hour is always before dawn. I can safely say that that is not the case. However, the coldest hour is definitely before dawn – especially when you are sitting on top of a mountain, wet from exertion and with a cold wind whistling around your privates.

As we sat and waited, Sapinggi told us the Duson legend as to how the mountain got its name. He said that long ago the Emporer of China heard that the most beautiful pearl on earth was hidden on the mountain. It was guarded by the most ferocious dragon in the world.

The emporer gathered his three sons together and told them that whichever one of them brought the pearl back would be the next Emporer. The first two sons failed but the third succeeded in snatching the pearl from the dragon. The dragon chased him and he hid in the forest below, where he married a beautiful Malay girl. When he returned to China with the pearl he forgot all about his wife. In her grief, she climbed to the top of the mountain and threw herself to her death. In memory of her desperate love, the mountain was named Kina (China) Balu (widow).

Sapinggi's fairy tale helped pass the time, and as he finished, the sky had begun to turn from black to a gravelly charcoal colour. As we watched, the first hint of orange crept over the horizon. From orange, the sky turned a dark red and the undersides of the clouds were flecked with gold.

As the sunrise developed into day, the chill began to leave my bones. I was beginning to enjoy myself. Somehow, inexplicably, the whole climb had seemed worthwhile, but as I walked back down to the guest house, I promised myself I would never climb a mountain to see the sunrise again. Well, not for a good long time anyway.

Riding A Typhoon On Ishigaki

An extract from A Ride In The Neon Sun, by Josie Dew

I landed at Tokyo's Narita airport with a bump and a bicycle and a handful of clichés about Japan: swarming armies of identically sombre-suited businessmen; houses which are more like hutches with no room to spare; pollution and Walkmen and yeses that mean no, entwined among inscrutable smiles and impenetrable speech and an enigmatic people whose names sound like makes of motorcycle.

Floating in my mind among these cliches were two indelible and disparate sounds that had spurred a sudden intrigue with Japan: *Madame Butterfly*, and a drum. Puccini's illustrious opera had always ruffled my feathers, tingled my spine and alluringly drifted in and out of my head. Then I set eyes and ears upon Kodo, a troupe of bewitching Japanese drummers powerfully unleashing themselves like coiled springs upon their traditional *taiko* drums, beating frenetically with a raw, naked and primal rhythm that resonated deeper than the heart and made me realise what the hairs on the back of my neck were for.

These two contrasting sounds – Italian opera and Japanese drum –

oscillated around my head until they merged and grew into a haunting crescendo full of nebulous titillation and a sudden stirring impulse that led me to Japan.

* * * * *

My senses were bombarded by the cacophony of an unaccustomed country. Arriving so suddenly, so unprepared, into a land so enigmatic was the price I had to pay for my spontaneous switch from my original plan to travel to New Zealand; and it left me reeling. I did not even know the basic words and phrases – I had planned on learning these on the plane but then I should have known that me and plans on planes are not a promising mix.

* * * * *

It had been another impossibly heavy and sultry grey ash-cloud sort of day, which culminated in an explosive storm just as I was racing through the rush-hour streets to catch the evening ferry. The storm clouds were so thick that a dreary daylight turned instantly to night. Headlights crawled through the ominous gloom as the roads turned to filthy black torrents of volcanic ash. By the time I arrived at the ferry terminal I was soaked and dirty.

A flurry of activity erupting from the crowd gathered around the ticket desk revealed that the Marix Line ferry might be delayed, due to a typhoon lurking somewhere in the direction of our destination. Fortunately the typhoon did an unexpected about-turn and so we slid out into the night, leaving the ash-blown lights of Kagoshima to flicker in our wake.

A grandmother wearing a Walkman and a girl in a 'We Love Sunny Day' T-shirt were my immediate neighbours in the 'Lady's Room', a long rectangular compartment which held at least thirty other women. This cheapest of accommodations contained no bunks or sheets or chairs but consisted merely of a raised expanse of carpeted floor (strictly no shoes) upon which lay rows of orange-brown blankets and plastic brown block-pillows shaped like bricks. The windows were sealed and

Riding A Typhoon On Ishigaki

the air was conditioned. A television gabbled away from a corner of the ceiling. It did not seem a recipe for a good night's slumber, so I extracted my ground sheet, Karrimat and sleeping bag and laid myself to rest in a leeward nook on deck beneath the stars.

Just as the first spokes of an early morning sun lit up a splintered pink sky, I rolled from the ship's ramp to land on the forty-mile-long volcanic island of Amami-Oshima. Weaving round a buzzing army of cargo-wielding forklifts, I entered the island's principal city of Naze. All was shut and quiet; I had the streets to myself. Palm trees rustled above my head and the warm air smelt exotically tropical.

When it comes to islands and countries that drive on the left, I will always cycle clockwise around their shores because it means I am riding right on the sea-side. To miss out on cycling inches away from precipitous cliffside drops that plummet into a raging and foaming ocean just because one is tucked to the inside of the road across two lanes of asphalt is not my idea of fun. I rode along the wharf, past a park and turned off on to an empty road that looped its way over the mountains to Ata. There was a truly wonderful descent spiralling down to a small fishing village full of bright blue tin-topped houses. With brilliant cobalt seas, coral reefs, palms, and crops of sago, papaya, bananas and sugarcane, it was not difficult to see why this subtropical archipelago had been labelled the Hawaii of Japan. It felt and smelt more like easygoing Polynesia than the robotic arm of Japan.

I came across a brand new tunnel, expensively bored through the mountainside for no more than a sleepy, single-track lane where the only traffic I had seen in two hours was an old man bumping along at about ten miles an hour on an ancient tractor, another old man on a back-firing moped with a front basket full of fish, and an elderly woman wearing on her back a basket loaded with brittle shrubbery and pushing a wheelbarrow piled with what looked like desiccated pineapple stalks.

I stopped at a small rural post office because I had discovered that post offices were one of the best sources of chilled water. In virtually every one in Japan I had found a metallic water-fountain machine that provided me with bottle-loads of refrigerated water. Some even had a help-yourself counter of iced *oolong cha*.

That night a sago farmer let me camp beside his *taka kura*, a traditional Amami thatched-roof wooden store-house set on stilts to keep rodents and vermin from eating the harvested grain. He said I was welcome to sleep inside it.

'Look', he said, sliding open the heavy wooden door and flicking a switch, 'there is *denki* – light – and also no danger from *habu*.'

'*Habu*?' I asked. 'What are *habu*?'

'*Abunai*! *Abunai*!' he replied, dramatically. '*Habu* are dangerous poisonous snakes!' Sweeping his arms in an elaborate arc to illustrate his point, he added, 'take care! *Habu* are everywhere!'

Okinawan snakes can grow up to six feet long – definitely not a tent mate with which a lone female wants to share her sleeping mat. But I did not know much about them then; I refused the sago farmer's offer of sleeping in a snake-free zone and merrily pitched my tent in the sandy dust across the path from the store-house. However, I did perform a rapid ten-second war-dance, stamping heavily on the ground in the hope that the vibrations would be sufficient to scare the snakes well away.

* * * * *

The meandering road up around Cape Kasarizaki was mountainous, sparse of life and truly spectacular. The first vehicle to pass me after a long time was a woman on a moped, her standard white-peaked, open-faced helmet worn on the back of her neck in carefree style. She motored alongside me for a couple of miles, laughing animatedly, shrieking above the spluttering strains of her engine, until she gestured to me to follow her down a bumpy track, its edges crowded with a windbreak of wild *fukugi* trees.

Her house, virtually hidden beneath a glorious tangle of cascading bougainvillea, hibiscus, ruby-red poinsettias, camellias, strings of white moon pearls, trumpet lilies and papaya trees, was in disarray and included twelve budgies, parrots, mynas and one very sniffy dog. I stayed with her for a couple of hours as she plied me with various edible delicacies and several litres of liquids. Before I left, she gave me a little drawstring bag her mother had made, one melon, a doggie-bag of fried

Riding A Typhoon On Ishigaki

eel, six rice balls and four cartons of fruit juice. Then she climbed on her moped and followed me at about five miles an hour all the way to the top of the mountain before bowing on her bike, smiling and waving, and heading back home.

I had not been on my own for long before a gun-metal Isuzu Big Horn jeep overtook me and stopped further up the road. A man in his thirties with wavy black hair and a face more Polynesian than Japanese gestured excitedly for me to stop. Iwai Kouichiro was a journalist from the island's daily paper and had briefly spotted me yesterday rolling out of Naze; he had been driving around the island looking for me ever since. 'A lady *gaijin* alone on a *jitensha*, on Amami Oshima – this is very strange sight', he said. Would I mind if he interviewed me? So we sat on the sea wall drinking Hokkaido beer as I tried to answer his questions in Japanese.

If I thought people had already been generous with their gift-giving, the next day was even more overwhelming. As I travelled back through Naze and then on over the mountains to the south of the island, everyone I met – shopkeepers, fishermen, petrol station attendants, roadworkers, car and lorry drivers – plied me with a phenomenal succession of gifts, because they had seen the picture of a *jitensha*-riding *gaijin* in the paper. My bike became a veritable mobile vending machine of refreshments.

By the time I arrived in Koniya, a bustling fishing town tucked into the magnificent Setouchi Coast, I was exhausted after a day of mountains, humidity and gift-accepting. It was almost dark. A fisherman told me that Koniya had a typhoon warning and I started looking for accommodation for the night. I was taken in by a roly-poly woman, whose family took me with them into the hot, humid night: the pink-paper-lantern-lit streets were alive with activity, people dressed in kimono and *happi* jackets happily clattering along in their clogs. Carrying platters of food and supplies of sake, we joined her husband on his small fishing boat and set off from the quay, motoring slowly out into the bay.

I had arrived in town just in time for Koniya's exuberant summer festival and tonight was the night for the spectacular show of *hanabi* – fire-flowers. Out in the bay we joined a flotilla of other small vessels bobbing engineless on a gently rolling swell. Their riggings were festooned with thousands of flickering lanterns, the kaleidoscopic reflections dancing off the face of the sea. A warm tropical breeze swept like silk across my bare shoulders, bringing with it faint odours of cigarettes, beer and fish. Our captain cut the engine and the sounds of chattering laughter drifted on the wind across the water. Sushi and *sake* went down the hatch, a mixture which, combined with the rousing distant deep beats of the traditional drum emanating from the shore, made me feel recklessly in love with Japan.

Then the fireworks started, set off from a barge moored off the shore. The sky exploded into wildly scintillating flowers of fire. Shrieks of delight erupted from boat after boat as continuous bursts of *hanabi* discharged and bloomed with a boom into an incandescent shower of radiating shapes that splintered the sky.

Not long after the grand finale, the wind whipped up and, with word of an approaching storm, everyone hurried for home.

I stayed in Koniya for over a week. It was one of those places where you occasionally arrive when everything feels right. It felt as if I had lived there for weeks. Sights and sounds and smells became very familiar: the early morning exercise music of the post office across the road (the workers, many with cigarette poised between their lips, synchronising their stretching movements in the loading yard); passing beneath my window, the dustbin lorry painted with swirls of bright flowers and playing loud, volume-distorted Chopin sonatas and Bach preludes from its exterior speaker (the rubbish collectors were all women, in dainty floral bonnets and frilly gloves); the sounds of the gossiping neighbours, mostly women, speed-talking but sounding like birds; the constant nonsensical nattering strains of television drifting through my windows, seeping through the walls; the wafts of frying fish floating on the air and the six o'clock sounds of a man across the alley breathing out luxurious moans of contentment as he sunk himself into his deep and indubitably scalding bath.

Riding A Typhoon On Ishigaki

Most days I would go on mini expeditions into the hills and mountains, where I would walk for hours feeling ridiculously happy.

* * * * *

A typhoon was upon me. I was on the island of Ishigaki at the time, camping on a beach. A fisherman woke me around 4.00am, warning me to seek shelter. I had more than a sneaking suspicion that this ancient fisherman knew what he was talking about and took his warning seriously. He conveyed the fact that it was still a good few hours away – time enough to find a roof over my head. I packed up, being careful to shake out both shoes and tent as this island was a famous *habu* haunt. (Indeed, as I wheeled off into a ferocious headwind the road was littered with tyre-squashed snakes. Not all the *habu* were lifeless: one, a six-foot monster with a body as thick as a drainpipe, snaked its way out of a cane field but rippled back from whence it had come when it caught sight of my startled form bearing down upon it.)

I battled north into the escalating gale along a narrow peninsula pounded on either side by horrendously huge and heaving seas to reach the small hamlet of Hirano where, the fisherman had informed me, I would find a *minshuku*. However, all I found was a ghost town of small, squat, concrete houses huddled behind heavy concrete walls with all their windows boarded up and not a soul in sight. Apart from the raking wind whining through the hamlet and the sound of a loose door banging back and forth on its hinges, the whole place was eerily quiet. Exhausted, I slumped jelly-legged on a kerbstone and began to shell some monkey nuts. No sooner had I placed nut number five in my mouth when a terrific thunderclap made me lose all contact with my skin. This dramatic detonation was enough to shake the ground like a small earthquake and reminded me that perching on the pavement shelling nuts was not wise in the face of an impending typhoon. Hurriedly I knocked on a few boarded-up doors but nobody was in. So I turned tail to race with the wind the sixteen kilometres back towards the junction at Ibaruma.

Charged up with a gush of adrenalin, my legs spun me southwards as the menacing sky detonated with head-shattering cracks all around me. Not one vehicle passed. Halfway down the rains began, alternating between torrentially vertical and torrentially horizontal, striking my skin like shards of glass. Within moments the road was hopelessly awash. Forked bolts of lightning cracked the black, bedevilled sky to pieces as I charged onwards. At one point I found myself with seas on either side so mountainous that they threatened to break clean across the waist-thin isthmus and sweep me into the East China Sea. The thunderous sky had merged with the furious ocean, blacking out the low ridge of mountains that formed the peninsula's spine.

Five kilometres from Ibaruma the wind picked up to such a buffeting pace that it was impossible to walk, let alone cycle. By the time I limped into town (a small cluster of houses lining the roadside) the late morning sky had caved in, turning day to tunnel-dark, with any objects that were not weighted down being hurled across the road. I narrowly missed decapitation by a metal sign torn from a lamp post and was momentarily winded by an airborne bucket taking me from behind.

I had to get inside, anywhere – and quick. Fighting my way into the wind, I hammered on the nearest boarded door with a no-nonsense degree of urgency. Moments later I was being dragged through a narrow crack by a small, dumpy woman with gold teeth. She took me under her ample and motherly wing and led me down a dark corridor to a small *tatami* room, dragged out a futon and a hard-husk pillow, showed me to the hot-tub and insisted on doing all my washing. Then she spread my table with tea things and a tray of tempura and rice.

To prevent the glass from being smashed, every window in the house was boarded up with sturdy wooden slats slotted into hefty steel girders built into the window frame.

By now the storm had whipped itself into such a fearsome tempest that what I had earlier taken to be a Herculean battle of the elements was nothing more than a damp and breezy sneeze. The terrific noise and violent velocity of the wind made me feel as if I was pinned to the side of a tunnel with a never-ending express train hurtling past my head.

Every now and then a gusty giant of a wind-devil slammed into the

Riding A Typhoon On Ishigaki

side of the house like gunshot. I peeped out through a slit in the window slats and saw a sheet of corrugated iron sail through the air like ricepaper before slicing a tree in two. When the electricity failed, my hostess appeared with a supply of candles and a thermos of hot water. With no electricity for the fan and being unable to open the windows, I found the air in my den suffocating and stiflingly humid. Sweat oozed freely.

As the ominous dark of day turned into night, the intensity of the wind increased to such a banging and bellowing howl that I felt certain the roof would be ripped clean off the house. All manner of objects continued to crash and smash outside my barricaded windows. All night the storm raged; it was impossible to sleep. By morning the clattering roar of the wind banging into the side of the house had increased to such an extent that it now felt as if my head was strapped inside a Jumbo jet's engine on take-off. The dark and violent scene through my window slit was of a cloaked and furious world caving in on itself.

I sat marooned on my futon island in an ever-dampening sea of *tatami*, counting raisins and peanuts by candle-light and really quite enjoying myself, apart from moments when I thought I might die with the next gust. Night two was no different to the previous one until around 2.00am when, suddenly, a complete and utter silence fell. I peered through the window. Not a breath of wind. Not a drop of rain. This sudden silence was eerie. The moon came and went as slithers of cloud drifted across its face. The storm had gone, blown itself out. A dog barked and a voice called to it – there was a world out there after all. My spirits soared and I padded back to bed, weary.

Twenty minutes later, THWAAM! The storm had returned, slamming so ferociously into the side of the house that the sliding partitions of my room collapsed on top of me. For the rest of the long night and even longer day the typhoon tugged and fought and wrestled with the island until finally, with only eight raisins, four peanuts, half a pineapple and a spoonful of honey to go, the seemingly endless storm gradually lessened its hold until it was no more than a very murky and savagely squally day.

After seventy-three hours in captivity, I emerged from my damp and wind-battered den to step once again into the Big Outdoors.

Planning to Travel...?

independent traveller's world

the world at your fingertips

- Over 200 specialist travel exhibitors
- Over 130 FREE travel talks
- Excellent value flights
- Job opportunities abroad
- Trekking & expeditions
- Specialist travel workshops
- Equipment and health advice
- Talk to experienced travellers

Annual Exhibitions

London Arena	5-7 February 1999
Glasgow, Scottish Exhibition Centre	27-28 February 1999
Manchester, G-Mex Centre	6-7 March 1999

freephone: 0800 328 0888 for details
entry from £5

The Imaginative Traveller

ACTIVE & ADVENTUROUS JOURNEYS

Wildlife, Mountains, Rivers & Deserts

16 different brochures to choose from

**Egypt, Middle East
Turkey, Omman
Yemen, Greece
Morocco, Africa**

**India, Nepal
China, Japan
South East Asia,
Central Asia
Trans Siberian**

**USA, Canada, Alaska
South & Central America**

Australia, New Zealand

Brochure Line **0181 742 3049**
Reservations 0181 - 742 8612

imaginative-traveller.com
ative-traveller.com
Passage, Chiswick, London W4 4PH

ATOL 3986

£1 OFF SINGLE DAY ENTRY